The Healthy Community
Moving Your Church Beyond Tunnel Vision

Dennis Bickers

BEACON HILL PRESS
OF KANSAS CITY

Copyright 2012 by Dennis Bickers and Beacon Hill Press of Kansas City

ISBN 978-0-8341-2797-5

Printed in the
United States of America

Cover design: J.R. Caines
Interior design: Sharon Page

Library of Congress Cataloging-in-Publication Data

Bickers, Dennis W., 1948-
   The healthy community : moving your church beyond tunnel vision / Dennis Bickers.
     p. cm.
   Includes bibliographical references (p.   ).
   ISBN 978-0-8341-2797-5 (pbk.)
   1. Church growth. 2. Church. 3. Mission of the church. 4. Church work. 5. Evangelistic work. 6. Non-church-affiliated people. I. Title.
   BV652.25.B53 2012
   262.001'7—dc23

2011042141

10 9 8 7 6 5 4 3 2 1

Dedication

Since 1966 I have been married to the most wonderful woman in the world. My life and ministry would have never been a tenth of what it's been without her love and support. We've been through more valleys and mountaintop experiences than either of us could have imagined when we married that fall day. There is no one I would have enjoyed the trip with more than her. Thank you, Faye, for everything. This book and my heart are dedicated to you.

Contents

Acknowledgments

Books do not happen automatically. Not only do they require a lot from the writer but also many others are responsible for them. I want to thank the region staff of the American Baptist Churches of Indiana and Kentucky, who allow me the time and freedom to write. I have never worked with a group of people who are more dedicated to their churches than the men and women who make up our staff.

As always, Beacon Hill Press has been great to work with as this book has come together. Bonny Perry is always so supportive and encouraging. Richard Buckner has worked with me on all five books I've done with Beacon Hill Press, and he's made each of them better with his questions and editing skills. He and the editing team, consisting of Sarah Glass, Ryan Pettit, and Kathy Baker, have worked hard to turn this manuscript into something worth reading, and I appreciate all of their efforts.

The one who sacrifices the most for my writing is my wife of forty-five years, Faye. She allows me to spend hours in my study researching and writing down my thoughts. She's always glad when I tell her I've finished a book, because I might start doing some things needing done around the house, but she also knows I probably have another one in mind that I'll soon start on. My life and my ministry would not be the same without her encouragement.

I would be remiss if I didn't mention those who actually purchase and read my books. I receive numerous emails telling me how much one of my books has helped a pastor or a church as it was addressing specific situations. I am amazed when I hear of churches ordering copies of one of my books for the entire congregation to study and the positive impact that study has on the life of the church. Judicatory leaders report they order copies for every pastor in their judicatory because they believe the material in those books will be a benefit to the pastor and his or her church. Such reports encourage me to continue writing and developing resources that will assist both church leaders and their churches.

Introduction

SINCE 1981 I have served as a Baptist minister. For the first twenty of those years I was the bivocational pastor of a small, rural church in Indiana, and in 2001 I became a judicatory minister in our denomination. As a result of previously written books, I have been privileged to lead workshops for various denominations in the United States and Canada. This has given me the opportunity to talk with the leaders of hundreds of churches, and it is interesting how many of them describe the same issues and challenges. Many of the pastors are discouraged and ready to leave the ministry. A pastor's wife told me recently how their oldest son despises the church his father serves and has even turned his back on God. Even many lay leaders are ready to abandon the church. Christian bookstores now have numerous books on their shelves that talk about how many people love Jesus Christ, but have little use for the church.

Jill Hudson tells us that 70 to 85 percent of unchurched people claim that "spirituality is important or very important to their lives."[1] Unfortunately, they do not believe that attending a church is important to their spiritual well-being. They listen to many of the television preachers and wonder if that is what the Christian faith is all about. Is Christianity really all about prosperity and having all your needs met? Can people really be healed simply by having the right preacher pray for them? If so, then why don't these television preachers go into the hospitals and empty the beds? And why

9

don't they go to the poorest of countries and explain to those people how they can become wealthy simply by asking, then believing that God will pour out blessings on them? Please understand these aren't necessarily my questions, as there are a number of excellent ministers on television who are reaching people with their preaching and their church's worship services. However, these are the kinds of questions unchurched people have asked me numerous times, and unfortunately, they are seldom satisfied with my answer.

Unchurched people also read about the battles going on within many of our denominations and wonder how those fit with the biblical commands to love one another. They hear the stories of local church fights and listen to church members complaining about their pastor or church at the local McDonald's and wonder why anyone would want to be involved in those churches. They may occasionally visit a church and leave wondering why anyone would want to spend their Sunday mornings there. The preaching lacked passion and had nothing to do with the issues they face. The worship service left them cold and confused. They came to experience God and see if he was real. They still don't know. It is very hard for them to see anything positive in the local church, so they stay away.

They are being joined by growing numbers of Christians who also see little benefit in attending church. These people are not leaving the church because they have lost their faith. They see the church as detrimental to their faith and harmful to their spiritual development.[2] George Barna's research has identified a group of Christians over twenty million strong that he calls "Revolutionaries." These are Christians who have left the established church for house churches and cyber churches. He explains their reasons for doing so.

They have no use for churches that play religious games, whether those games are worship services that drone on without the presence of God or ministry programs that bear no spiritual fruit. Revolutionaries eschew ministries that compromise or soft sell our sinful nature to expand organizational turf. They refuse to follow people in ministry leadership positions who cast a personal vision rather than God's, who seek popularity rather than the proclamation of truth in their public statements, or who are more concerned about their own legacy than that of Jesus Christ. They refuse to donate one more dollar to man-made monuments that mark their own achievements and guarantee their place in history. They are unimpressed by accredited degrees and endowed chairs in Christian colleges and seminaries that produce young people incapable of defending the Bible or unwilling to devote their lives to serving others. And Revolutionaries are embarrassed by language that promises Christian love and holiness but turns out to be all sizzle and no substance.[3]

What Has Gone Wrong?

The church is the body of Christ (see Col. 1:24), and Jesus Christ said that "the gates of hell [would] not prevail against it" (see Matt. 16:18, KJ21), but something has definitely gone wrong since those words were spoken. I believe the church has developed a disease over the years that is slowly killing it along with its ability to impact society and transform lives. We will cover a number of contributing factors in this book: lack of biblical authority, lack of grace for one another, a maintenance mentality that prefers the status quo over change, failure of pastoral leadership, failure to disciple new believers, lack of denominational support, and failure to properly understand the mission of the church.

As one might guess from reading the above list, there will be something in this book that could offend almost everyone, but that is not my intention. It is my desire to speak truthfully about the problems that exist in too many of our churches today, in the hope that God's people will honestly examine themselves and their churches to see if they exhibit these symptoms.

Why Write This Book?

Like many people, I am concerned about our nation and the world in which we live. Now more than ever, we are impacted by events in other parts of the world. As I write this, new countries such as North Korea and Iran are developing nuclear weapons, wars are going on in various places, and there are economic problems that have cost millions of people their jobs, their homes, and much of their retirement funds. Personal debt is in the billions of dollars, and the national debt is even higher.

Numerous other social issues also impact peoples' lives. Drug abuse, alcoholism, the rise in single-parent homes, AIDS and other sexually transmitted diseases, increased poverty levels, abortion, racism, sexism, and ageism are just a few. The great shame of too many of our churches today is that they are silent on these issues. Multitudes of people want someone to help them make sense of the issues in their lives, and the church needs to seize the opportunity. The first decade of the twenty-first century has presented the church an open window to share the hope of the gospel with people who have no hope, and most of our churches are missing this opportunity. Too many of us are so focused on our own needs and the preservation of our churches that we have abandoned society and forced it to seek answers elsewhere.

One of the reasons many people today are not involved in a local church is that they believe the church is irrelevant to the needs and issues of the twenty-first century. They believe we are answering questions that no one is asking anymore, and too often they are right. They see nothing *in* the church and hear nothing *from* the church that appeals to them or helps them make sense of their lives, so they look elsewhere to satisfy their spiritual hunger.

I wrote this book because I believe the Bible does address the issues faced by people today. The message the church has to proclaim is just as relevant to the struggles of people today as it was when it was first given. It is not the Bible or the gospel message that has become irrelevant. What has become irrelevant is the manner in which too many churches have chosen to do ministry today. Our churches have abandoned their reason for existing.

I am certainly not the first to say this, but I see little hope for our world unless the church recaptures its God-given purpose and begins to once again impact our communities. There can be no revival in a nation or even in a community unless there is first a revival in the church. Second Chronicles 7:14 makes this very clear: "If My people who are called by My name will humble themselves, and pray and seek My face, and turn from their wicked ways, then I will hear from heaven, and will forgive their sin and heal their land."

It is easy to point the finger of blame at various groups for the problems that plague our society, but God makes it clear in the above passage that he will heal the land when his people (the church) repent from their evil ways. He's not waiting on the drug lord or the racist to repent. He's not waiting for the politicians to begin governing according to biblical principles and values. He is waiting for the church to repent for failing to be the church he created us to be and to recapture the purpose for its existence. He is waiting for the church to once again become a light set on a hill. But none of this will happen unless the church first experiences a healing of its heart.

Be Filled with Hope for Your Church

This book is mostly about hope. I want pastors and lay leaders to recapture the belief that their church can make a difference in the life of their communities. It is my prayer that every church leader reading this book will make an honest appraisal of the condition of his or her church and begin to look for ways to help it become healthier. This is not a book to beat up, but a book to lift up. God wants to use your church to make a difference in the lives of men, women, and young people in your community. You might have to make major changes in your church, but it will be worth whatever pain those changes create because your church will once again make a difference in people's lives.

part 1

The Problem

1

A Lack of Biblical Authority

It is an immense irony that a generation that has
access to the best in biblical exegesis is,
even among the so-called "educated clergy,"
so largely indifferent to it.[1]

—Eugene Peterson

THE MOST IMPORTANT decision that a church or individual can make is deciding what to believe about the Bible. This is a strong statement, and some readers will disagree. Some will argue that the most important decision that a person will ever make involves their relationship with Jesus Christ. I certainly agree that this decision is the most important decision a person can make as it relates to eternal life, but I would counter that until a person first decides what he or she believes about the Bible, that person cannot make a proper decision about what to do with Jesus Christ.

Our postmodern society wants to include the Bible with the books of other religions. They see Christianity as just one of many religious options to choose from, and they are all equally valid. Jesus Christ is viewed as a great prophet, teacher, or religious leader, but many in today's postmodern society do not believe he is any different from the leaders of other religions. The problem with this view is that Christ does not give us that option. In John 14:6 Jesus exclaims, "I am the way, the truth, and the life. No one comes to the Father except through Me." C. S. Lewis explained what this means to us.

> I am trying here to prevent anyone saying the really foolish thing that people often say about Him: "I'm ready to accept Jesus as a great moral teacher, but I don't accept His claim to be God." That is the one thing we must not say. A man who was merely a man and said the sort of things Jesus said would not be a great moral teacher. He would either be a lunatic—on a level with the man who says he is a poached egg—or else he would be the Devil of Hell. You must make your choice. Either this man was, and is, the Son of God: or else a madman or something worse. You can shut him up for a fool, you can spit at Him and kill Him as a demon; or you can fall at His feet and call Him Lord and God.

But let us not come up with any patronizing nonsense about His being a great human teacher. He has not left that open to us. He did not intend to.[2]

Lewis clearly explains that considering all the Scriptures say about Jesus Christ, we are left with a trilemma. Either Jesus Christ is Lord, a lunatic, or a liar. What we believe about the Bible will determine which of the three we consider Christ to be. Is the Word of God given to us in order to reveal God and his purposes for our lives? Or is it merely a book about God that was written by human beings to teach ethical and moral truths that lead to a better society?

What Does the Bible Say?

Christians approach the Bible differently. Some believe it is without error in every detail, while others affirm it to be without error in all things necessary to salvation. There are also Christians who hold variations of these views. But no matter which opinion you accept, the issue at stake is the Bible's authority. We may disagree about how a certain passage of Scripture should be understood, but once the meaning is determined, we are obligated to conform to it because it is God's revelation of himself to us. A Christian ought not respond, "So what?" when confronted by the teachings of Scripture.

With that said, let's look at two passages that reveal the apostles' view of Scripture. In 2 Timothy 3:16-17, Paul claims, "All Scripture is given by inspiration of God, and is profitable for doctrine, for reproof, for correction, for instruction in righteousness, that the man of God may be complete, thoroughly equipped for every good work." The phrase "given by inspiration of God" literally means "God-breathed."

I personally do not hold to the dictation theory that says God dictated the Bible word for word to the various writers. I believe the writers wrote from their experiences with God, and that God inspired their writings in such a way as to reliably convey the truth about himself. This will be seen more clearly in the next passage, but before we go there, notice the purpose of the Scriptures. The apostle Paul clearly explains that they are given to us to enable every believer in Jesus Christ to grow in his or her faith. The words of Scripture are profitable to each of us as they reveal God's purpose for our lives, and they give us practical guidance for how we should live our lives. If Scripture comes from God and is meant to serve the purposes mentioned above, it is clear that they are intended to be authoritative for our belief and practice.

The second passage is 2 Peter 1:20-21. "Knowing this first, that no prophecy of Scripture is of any private interpretation, for prophecy never came by the will of man, but holy men of God spoke as they were moved by the Holy Spirit."

In this passage, Peter teaches us that the writers of Scripture did not simply write down words; they wrote as they were inspired by the Spirit of God. There is also a helpful word picture here. In New Testament times, boats were moved by the wind blowing on their sails. Similarly, the words of Scripture we read today were inspired by God as he moved in the hearts and minds of its authors. Ultimately, according to these passages, God is the author of the Bible.

There are other scriptures we could look at, but for some people there could never be enough scripture to convince them that God is the author of the Bible. They have convinced themselves otherwise, and they are highly resistant to changing their mind. Unfortunately, as we will see later in this chapter, a large number of Christians, including many clergy, have decided the Bible is not the Word of God, but merely a collection of stories designed to teach moral truths.

What About the Errors in the Bible?

It is not the purpose of this book to present a defense of the Bible, but we will briefly address one common question that causes people to doubt the authority of the Bible. People who do not want to accept the Bible as the authoritative Word of God usually speak of errors or contradictions in the text. The next time someone says that to you, get out your Bible and ask him or her to point out one to you. Very few people will ever be able to do so because they've never studied the Scriptures for themselves; they have just accepted what someone else told them.

It must be admitted that there are variations in some of the ancient manuscripts, but the vast majority of these involve grammatical construction, the spelling of words, and other trivial differences.[3] Frederic Kenyon states emphatically that "no fundamental doctrine of the Christian faith rests on a disputed reading."[4] We should also note that not one archaeological discovery has ever proven the Bible wrong.[5] However, archaeology has often proven the skeptics and critics wrong.

A prime example of this involves the Gospel of Luke and the book of Acts. For many years, some scholars questioned the accuracy of Luke's writings and pointed to numerous "errors." One mistake they believed Luke made is when he referred to Lysanias as a tetrarch in Abilene around A.D. 27 (see Luke 3:1). The scholars pointed out that Lysanias was actually the ruler of Chalcis five decades earlier, and Luke's writings became suspect. These critics insisted that if Luke was wrong about this he might be wrong about other things he recorded. However, archaeologists later found an inscription dated from A.D. 14 to 37 that named Lysanias as tetrarch in Abila. There had been two persons named Lysanias, and Luke's record was correct.[6]

Of course, archaeology can only prove whether something is correctly described or historically accurate. It cannot prove or disprove spiritual truths. Its value lies in challenging those who insist the Bible is historically inaccurate or that it contains errors. Each person still must decide for himself or herself whether to believe the Bible is the Word of God or that it is merely a book about God like any other book.

Why Is This Important?

Does it really matter if we believe the Bible is the inspired Word of God? I believe it does matter because it is from the Bible that the church receives its message. If we believe the Bible was simply written by a group of men with typical human frailties and motivations and is therefore unreliable and not authoritative, then how can we know that what the Bible says about salvation is accurate? John 3:16 assures us that "God so loved the world that He gave His only begotten Son, that whoever believes in Him should not perish but have everlasting life." This tremendous promise has brought hope to millions of people who have decided to put their faith in Jesus Christ. But, if the Bible does not truly convey God's word to us, how do we know for certain that this passage isn't erroneous? Maybe salvation isn't for "whoever believes in Him" but is only for left-handed, blue-eyed people living in Europe.

This is a practical matter as well. If the Bible is not authoritative, then why should we obey it? Why should we follow its moral principles? Many who reject the full authority of Scripture do so precisely because they want to follow their own morality. However, without moral absolutes a society will soon find itself in utter chaos. Who is to say that murder or rape or stealing is wrong? Some will argue that our consciences will tell us that such actions are wrong, but can we trust our consciences? Read any newspaper and see how moral our society's behavior is when it just follows its conscience.

Our postmodern society claims it does not believe in absolute truth; therefore, the Bible cannot be true. To the postmodern thinker, the Bible is "true" for those who believe it is true, but its teachings should not be forced on those who do not accept it. This rejection of absolute truth confuses me. How can someone insist that something is true for one person, but another person can hold an opposite belief that must be considered equally accurate? In addition, if one claims there is no such thing as absolute truth, is that not a statement of absolute truth? David Berlinski answers that question by saying, "If it is, then some truths are absolute after all, and if some are, why not others? If it is not, just why would we pay it any mind, since its claims on our attention will vary according to circumstances?"[7]

One of my favorite classes in college was logic, and one of the primary laws of logic is the law of noncontradiction. In simple language, this law states that a claim cannot be both true and not true at the same time. If I tell you there is a brown desk in my study, the statement is either true or it is not true. It cannot be both. I happen to be sitting in front of a brown desk in my study as I type these words, so I know it is true. If you doubt my statement, it is easy to verify. All you have to do is to come into my study. If you choose to not believe me or come to my study to verify my statement, that doesn't make my statement false and yours true. In fact, you would be wrong. Whether or not you believe it is immaterial to the truth of my claim.

Let's apply this same thinking to Jesus' statements in John 3:16 and in John 14:6, two scriptures we have previously mentioned. If one believes in an authoritative Bible, then one must believe that Jesus' statements in both passages of Scripture are true. As apologist Ravi Zacharias writes, "Jesus' absolute claim that He is the way, the truth, and the life means categorically that anything that contradicts what He says is by definition false."[8] Two competing religious systems that contradict each other cannot both be true. They can both be false or one can be true and the other false, but both cannot be true. It is important to admit that if your religious beliefs are true and they are contrary to biblical teaching, then the Bible must be false, and the millions of people who have accepted its teachings have been deceived. However, if my beliefs are true, you are the one who is deceived. There is no easy, middle ground where both can be equally true.

Now do you see why I say the most important decision you can make is what to believe about the Bible? It is the key to reliable information about who Jesus is and how we should live. I have staked my life and my eternal destiny on the truth and authority of the Bible.

The Bible was under attack long before postmodernism declared there is no absolute truth, and the reasons for those attacks has not changed. Though some people challenge the authority of the Bible for intellectual reasons, many do so primarily to protect the lifestyle choices they have made. If they admit that the Bible is true, then God does exist and the Bible's moral teachings must be obeyed. Their lives will have to change or they will face the judgment of God. These skeptics do not want the God of the Bible; they want a god created in their own image. They prefer a belief system that fits their lifestyle rather than subject their lifestyle to God and his Word. I can understand unchurched people wanting to do this. What I can't understand is why so many in today's church want to join in this self-deception.

Christians and the Bible

George Barna reports that 79 percent of born-again American adults believe that the Bible is accurate in all the principles it teaches. That means 21 percent, over one-fifth, believe that the Bible teaches principles that should not be followed. Only 40 percent of born-again adults believe that Satan is a real force, despite all the Bible teaches about him. Although the Bible teaches that Jesus Christ lived a sinless life on earth, only 62 percent of born-again adults strongly believe that teaching.[9] These are frightening statistics. The teachings of Scripture are at the very heart of the Christian faith. If people claiming to be born-again Christians reject the truth of biblical teachings, they reject or distort the heart of the gospel message.

The figures become even more alarming when we look at how clergy in the mainline churches view Scripture. In a 2008 survey of mainline Protestant clergy conducted by Public Religion Research, 67 percent responded they did not believe the Bible was the inerrant Word of God in matters of faith and in historic, geographical, and other secular matters.[10] The word *inerrant* is a loaded word that may have affected the responses to the question, but it is still significant that two-thirds of the ministers who responded to this survey lacked confidence in Scripture to some degree. Unfortunately, the view of Scripture that is in the pulpit will likely be the same view held in the pew.

The apostle Peter warned the church that false teachers will rise up, bringing destructive heresies that would lead many into error (see 2 Pet. 2:1-3). These false teachers will be successful because some in the church will prefer false teaching over sound doctrine. Those with "itching ears" will seek out false teaching (see 2 Tim. 4:3-4) because it does not threaten their moral and ethical choices. There is no danger of being convicted of sin because such teachers never speak of sin or judgment. They assure their listeners that God is only interested in blessing them. As a result, we see little difference in the lives of many Christians compared to the lives of those who do not claim to be Christians.

A Watered-down Gospel

Christians do not know how to live because they don't know what to believe, and they often don't know what to believe because of the messages they hear each week from their pulpits. When pastors have a low view of Scripture, they are unlikely to present a strong, biblical message. They may discuss the current issue of the day or share from an article they have read in a secular magazine, but they have nothing authoritative to say.

A friend once shared with me about a time when he struggled with alcohol. He knew he needed help to conquer his problem and decided to talk to a pastor. Since he didn't personally know a pastor at that time, he made an appointment with the pastor of one of the larger churches in his community. After his appointment, his wife asked how it went. He responded that the pastor really didn't say anything to help him overcome his drinking problem, but he did try to make him feel better about himself. He laughingly told me later that the pastor did everything he could to make him feel better about being a drunk!

It wasn't until a later meeting with another pastor who showed my friend from the Scriptures how much God loved him and provided forgiveness and salvation through Jesus Christ that he was able to conquer his problem with alcohol. The first pastor did not allow Scripture to speak authoritatively to the problem. This reflects a low view of Scripture. The second pastor did not hesitate to take my friend directly to the Scriptures. Because of his confidence in them, and because he believed what he read in the Bible, my friend experienced victory through the power of Christ.

Some churches believe they need to water down their gospel presentation in order not to offend people or in an effort to attract new people to their services. There are few references to the Scriptures in their worship services, and some subjects are avoided completely. Their pastors fear that if they present a sermon based too strongly on the authority of the Bible that they would lose their congregations. Yet, if that was the case, how did Billy Graham consistently fill up stadiums night after night? Time after time in his sermons he would begin a statement with, "The Bible says . . ." And he said it with an audible conviction that proved he believed what the Bible said. Millions of lives were changed because Billy Graham confronted people with the truths found in Scripture.

The fear of losing people is completely unfounded. Thom Rainer's research of formerly unchurched people found that "we should never dilute biblical teaching for the sake of the unchurched."[11] He found that 91 percent of formerly unchurched people reported that doctrine was one of the important factors that attracted them to the church they eventually joined.[12] Journalist Colleen Carroll's year-long study of young adults led her to report that a number of them are turning to orthodox Christianity because "they have been exposed to 'watered-down' religion, moral relativism, or atheism, and they crave its opposite."[13] She states that these young adults "embrace challenging faith commitments that offer them firm guidelines on how to live their lives."[14]

Churches do not have to dilute the gospel in order to attract people. In fact, one reason that some avoid going to church is because its message is so diluted, it's not worth getting out of bed to hear it. People want to hear what God has to say about the issues that trouble them most. The Sunday after September 11, 2001, many churches reported large crowds of visitors. People were frightened and confused. For many of them, it was the first time they had entered a church in years. In their fear and pain, they attended a worship service to hear if God had anything to say about the recent events. Within a few weeks, most churches reported that their attendance had returned to pre-9/11 numbers. Why did this happen? Perhaps people decided that God could not help with the fear, pain, and confusion they were feeling. Perhaps it reinforced what many believed: the church is irrelevant to their lives. The church needs to seize golden opportunities like this to reach people who are hungry for words of hope and encouragement from Scripture, but too many churches miss it because they dilute the Word of God.

The Bible Is Relevant to Real Issues

As mentioned in the introduction, people are hurting due to the overwhelming social and financial pressures they are facing. America is facing the worst financial situation since the Great Depression, and it's not just America that is hurting. Virtually every economic system in the world has been impacted by this financial meltdown. A number of causes for this crisis have been identified: greed, excessive credit, lack of savings, and poor loans made by lending institutions are among the most commonly cited. Where do people turn for answers to problems like these?

Walk into any bookstore and you will find an array of books to help people through this economic downturn. They will tell you how to avoid foreclosure, what to do if you lose your job, how to invest in bad economic times, how to live on less, and how you can become rich. There is nothing necessarily wrong with most of these books, and one could assume the theories in each book worked for its author. However, there is one ancient book that contains great wisdom about finances that won't be found on the shelf with the others, and that book is the Bible.

In 1991, the late Larry Burkett warned that America would soon encounter a serious financial crisis.[15] As he wrote, the country was in a recession, but he believed that the economy would go through at least one more cycle and possibly two before encountering a major meltdown. The factors he believed would cause this crisis were consumer debt, federal debt, a banking crisis, business failures, and a denial by leaders that anything is wrong. Does any of this sound familiar?

Near the end of his book, Burkett asked, "'Will Christians be a part of the solution . . . or a part of the problem?' As of this minute I would say that most Christians in America are as much a part of the problem as anyone else. There is basically no difference in how the average Christian handles his or her finances compared to the average non-Christian."[16] Burkett went on to say that many Christians consistently violate biblical principles in the areas of finances, observing that they overspend their earnings, fail to save for the future, and so on.

Those who claim the Bible is irrelevant to their lives have simply never heard what the Bible says about finances, and the reason they haven't heard is that many churches haven't taken the time to teach the financial principles found in the Bible. Some who claim to do so teach a "prosperity gospel" that is far removed from what the Bible actually teaches. For years, Larry Burkett and Ron Blue provided resources that could be used in churches to teach biblical principles on finances, but few churches ever used them. Dave Ramsey now offers his Financial Peace University, and a number of churches are now using that program to teach biblical principles to their members and to the larger community. Let's pray that more churches do so in the future.

Of course, the Bible speaks of more than just finances. It contains God's instructions regarding family life and marriage. It addresses racism, sexism, and ageism. The Bible warns against exploiting the poor and defenseless and insists that all people are to be treated justly and with compassion. It helps us make decisions that are ethically and morally sound. In short, it teaches us how to live, and the world would be a much better place if the teachings found in the Bible were practiced by each of us. Far from being irrelevant, the Bible contains the only way of life that is worth living.

The Bible Speaks to the Church

An authoritative Bible gives purpose and meaning to the church. Many churches today operate without any clear sense of mission and purpose. They develop programs, fill up their calendars, and accomplish very little. They chase fads instead of focusing on the ministry God has given them to do. This issue will be addressed in detail in chapter 3, but for now we can say that the root cause of many churches' failure to understand their purpose and mission is because of their weak view of the Bible.

The mission of the church is very clear. We find it in the Great Commission (see Matt. 28:19-20) and the Great Commandment (see 22:36-40). The church is to be engaged in evangelism and in serving those in need. Unfortunately, we see little effective evangelism done in churches today. Too many of them are only interested in meeting the needs of their members, not in ministering to those outside the church. Such churches take neither the Great Commission nor the Great Commandment seriously because they do not take the Bible seriously. Former Southern Baptist president James Draper said it well: "There is no example in history of a church or a denomination which became more and more zealous for genuine biblical evangelism and missions while at the same time becoming less biblical in its theology and moving away from the authority of Scripture."[17]

If the Bible is true, then people without a personal relationship with Jesus Christ are lost and will be eternally separated from God when they die (John 14:6). If the Bible is really true, then we are all sinners who need forgiveness from our sins (see Rom. 3:23). We are not sinful because we sin; we sin because we are sinful. There is a difference, and the Bible teaches that we are all born sinful. Furthermore, the Bible teaches that our sins have separated us from God. However, the good news is that anyone who wants to receive God's forgiveness and become a child of God is invited to do so (see John 3:16). All of these things are taught by Scripture. If we regard the Bible as authoritative, we are not free to replace these things with ideas that are more appealing. We must believe that the biblical description of the problem of sin and its remedy is true. This makes sense of Jesus' commands to engage in evangelism. If a church is not involved in evangelistic outreach, it can only mean that it does not believe what the Bible says about man's condition without Christ. It has made some other source of theology more authoritative than Scripture.

Denominations and the Bible

Doctrinal confusion is also one of the reasons why so many denominations are struggling today. Mainline denominations have struggled for years with two issues that have greatly divided their churches: abortion and homosexuality. Many of their national gatherings spend time addressing these issues with heated discussion from both sides. Those who hold to more liberal views on these subjects will claim that culturally defined social justice requires that women be given the right to an abortion and that same-sex couples should be allowed to marry. Conservatives point to various scriptures that speak against both practices. Which side has the strongest argument? Do the popular ideas of our current culture trump biblical authority? These are the questions denominations need to answer. For me, biblical authority is greater than cultural trends, autonomy of the local church, or any of the other arguments brought up in such debates.

The problem is that denominational leaders straddle the fence in an effort to please both sides. They are caught between wanting to be "relevant" or "current" and wanting to avoid discipline from denominational authorities. Or perhaps they are caught between wanting to have a bigger congregation and a desire to be faithful to the Word of God. If they are honest, they will recognize that fence-straddling only slows the problem, it doesn't stop it.

I serve in one of the denominations that has debated these two issues for many years. As a judicatory minister, I have met with numerous churches to explain our denomination's position on the issue of homosexuality. Few churches were satisfied with that position because it seemed that the denominational leadership was unwilling to resist cultural trends in favor of biblical teaching. Recently, an entire region withdrew from the denomination over its failure to address homosexuality from a biblical perspective. Other congregations have decided to become independent or join other denominations. Fortunately, some of our churches still take a biblical stance on this issue. Their solution is to remain connected with our judicatory while distancing themselves from the denomination by reallocating their mission support. However, as a result fewer dollars are now going into the denomination's general fund. A number of people have lost their jobs and some missionaries are at risk of being recalled.

This is a great example of the way a rejection of biblical authority leads to another problem: the loss of ministry opportunities. We have spent enormous amounts of time, energy, and financial resources discussing these issues instead of investing those resources in opportunities to do ministry. These losses have occurred at both a national level and locally as well.

Missionaries whose funding is drying up as a result of these debates are distracted from the work to which God has called them. They are forced to spend valuable time and money on raising their own funds in order to remain in the field.

Finally, the ones most hurt by the doctrinal confusion that exists in many of our denominations are the people for whom Jesus Christ gave his life. They are consistently confronted with a weak, ineffective church that doesn't appear to know what it believes instead of having the opportunity to encounter the living Christ who could bring change into their lives.

Summary

Ed Stetzer and Elmer Towns list several core doctrines that are essential to Christianity, and one of these is the authority of the Scriptures. They write, "Take away the authority of the Bible, or the essential content of the Bible, and you no longer have Christianity."[18] You may have a good organization or belief system that does many good things, but you have something less than the Christian faith. Without an authoritative Bible, the church will be susceptible to a variety of popular, yet false beliefs. People will pick and choose which ideas to dismiss and which ideas to add until their "Christianity" is unrecognizable as the apostolic faith. Those who create their own version of Christianity in this way have no solid foundation upon which to offer truth because their source is considered unreliable and open to change with cultural trends. We are no longer anchored to truth when we believe one person's theology is just as true as another's no matter how those two theologies may disagree. We need Scripture to settle theological disagreements and provide a trustworthy foundation for belief. Someone has said the primary belief system in our postmodern world can be summed up in one word: "Whatever." Without an authoritative Bible, the same will be true of the church as well.

The legitimacy of everything we preach and believe depends on its relationship to the Scripture. If we cannot believe that the Scripture is true, then we have no solid basis to proclaim its message. That is why I began this book by addressing the problem of doctrinal confusion, and it's why I said the most important decision you or your church will ever make is what to believe about the Bible.

An authoritative Bible is at the heart of everything we do as a church. It informs our mission and purpose and provides direction for how we are to live our lives. When a church decides that the Bible is not the inspired Word of God and may be edited to suit current tastes, it undermines the source of its own authority as well. It has nothing to offer humankind but a repackaged mishmash of feel-good, secular humanism. It will drift along accomplishing little or nothing for the kingdom of God. For churches to effectively minister in the twenty-first century, they must deal with this doctrinal confusion and lack of agreement that is sending harmful mixed signals to the world.

2
A Jack of Grace

Woe to you, scribes and Pharisees, hypocrites!
For you are like whitewashed tombs which indeed
appear beautiful outwardly, . . . but inside you
are full of hypocrisy and lawlessness.
—Matthew 23:27-28

THE ONLY PEOPLE Jesus condemned during his time on this earth were the hypocritical religious leaders who refused to practice what they preached. Jesus never spoke a word of condemnation to the Samaritan woman he met at the well who had been married five times and was then living with a man to whom she was not married. To the woman who had been caught in the act of adultery Jesus said, "Neither do I condemn you; go and sin no more" (John 8:11). While passing through Jericho, Jesus spent the day in the home of Zacchaeus, a despised tax collector. While others pointed out that Jesus was spending the day with a sinner, Zacchaeus experienced the grace of God and repented of his sins. That day, Jesus said, salvation came to Zacchaeus (see Luke 19:1-10). Jesus repeatedly offered forgiveness and grace to all he encountered and reserved his words of judgment for the religious leaders who made life difficult for those who sought to experience God in their lives. I wonder what he would say to some of us in the church today.

Where Is the Grace Today?

As a judicatory leader, I often see a serious lack of grace in our churches. I know a church whose board handed their pastor a request for his resignation as he was greeting people following their Easter service. Another church had a pastor whose teenage daughter became pregnant. A few weeks after this discovery the pastor went into the hospital, and while there, a delegation from the church visited him requesting he resign or be terminated. In a third church, the leaders told the pastor they wanted his immediate resignation at the upcoming business meeting, and if he gave it they would provide him with three months' severance pay and he could remain in the parsonage for that three months. He did submit his resignation at that meeting, and when the meeting ended they told him they had changed their mind and would only give him two months' severance and two months in the parsonage. Within a week or two they changed the locks on the doors of the church so his key wouldn't work. In none of these instances had the pastor committed any grievous offense that warranted such behavior from the church. The resignation requests could have been handled with more grace on the part of the church.

Not only do we treat our church leaders with little grace; we show little grace to one another. A number of years ago a young girl made a profession of faith at a vacation Bible school. The church pastor and I visited the girl's mother and asked her opinion of her daughter's decision. She was pleased that her daughter had become a Christian, but she was not pleased that her daughter wanted to be baptized. She wanted to know if that meant her daughter would become a member of our church. She then told us that she had once been a member of another church in the community. She had been very active in that church until her husband decided to divorce her. The next Sunday she went to church as always, but something was different. It seemed to her that the temperature in that church had dropped ten degrees. Former friends shunned her as if she had a communicable disease. After being treated like that for a few weeks she stopped attending and had never returned to church. She didn't want her daughter to be hurt by church members as she had been.

In another church there were two families who seemed to keep things stirred up all the time. New people would come into the church but leave within a few months because of the actions of one of these families. One time, one of the couples approached a new Christian who was a single mother trying to raise four children. They told this struggling mother all she was doing wrong with her children. She never returned to that church. Why would she? She had enough struggles in her life. She needed love and support from her new church family, not more criticism. I have seen similar scenarios played out in many churches, driving people away from the church and from God.

A bivocational pastor I was coaching told me she had often thought of forming a ministry in her church to reach out to people who had been hurt by the church. She wanted to know if I felt such a ministry could be successful. I assured her if she developed an effective ministry to that group of people, her church would not remain small for long. Every community has many such people.

Unfortunately, our lack of grace is also felt by those outside the church, and they are repelled by it. One young lady explained her attitude about Christianity and the church by pointing to a friend of hers.

Before my friend became a Christian you could talk to him. He was normal. He became a Christian after he met a girl, and then through her got converted. But after his conversation, you couldn't talk to him anymore. Every conversation was about condemning something about my lifestyle. All he did was keep telling me all the things I was doing wrong. I shouldn't be smoking. I shouldn't be drinking. He didn't like the way I dressed or the music I listened to. I was mad at the church for turning him into this kind of very negative person. You ask why I don't go to church? Why would I want to become a negative person like most Christians are? That's why. The world is negative enough without having the church make me more negative. I saw what it did to someone very close to me, and I don't want to become like that.[1]

Some might argue that not all Christians are like that, but the fact is that some are, and too often all Christians are judged by the bad behavior of a few. We become better known for what we oppose than what we stand for. Members of one church carry signs saying that God hates homosexuals. They protest at military funerals, claiming that the deaths are God's punishment for America's protection of homosexuals. Some non-Christians see this on the news and assume all churches think like this.

Jesus once condemned the Pharisees for the impossible standards they established for the Sabbath (see Mark 2:23—3:5). They had turned the Sabbath into something God never intended by adding man-made rules and imposing them upon the people. What would Jesus say about some of our man-made rules that we try to impose on people?

There are churches that still fight over which version of the Bible is the true version. In the twenty-first century there are still Christians who condemn men whose hair is longer than these Christians believe is proper. I talked with members of one church who were so opposed to women teaching men that they did not allow books by a well-known female Christian leader to be in their church library. In some circles women are condemned for wearing makeup or having the wrong hairstyle. I heard a preacher respond to that one time by saying that if your God isn't bigger than a tube of lipstick, you need a new God.

We condemn young people for tattoos and piercings, but where is the biblical justification for such condemnation? A verse in Leviticus forbidding tattoos was speaking against a pagan custom honoring the false gods that existed in the nations surrounding Israel. Many tattoos today are merely artistic expressions honoring a significant event in one's life, such as marriage, the birth of a child, the loss of a loved one, or to honor something of value. I have seen Christians with tattoos who expressed their faith to all who saw them.

Some Christians condemn fellow believers if they drive an expensive car, live in a nice home, or wear fine clothing. I once had a church member tell me she hoped she would never see me driving a Cadillac. I assured her that would not happen because if I could afford a Cadillac, I would probably buy a Mercedes. She was not pleased.

Even if you follow all the rules that others try to force on you, it is still possible to get into trouble with the legalists if you associate with others who don't follow those rules. Jack Van Impe enjoyed great success as an evangelist conducting city-wide crusades. Multitudes of people received Jesus Christ as their Lord and Savior as a result of attending his crusades. However, in the late 1970s he began to receive criticism for associating with persons not acceptable to certain fundamentalist leaders. When he refused to renounce those associations, these leaders withdrew their support from him and sent letters around the country asking that pastors and other leaders refuse to support him since he had abandoned his fundamentalist roots.[2]

Of course, Van Impe is not the only Christian leader who has been criticized for not separating himself from those whom some people consider liberal or moderate. When Jerry Falwell formed the Moral Majority, he invited Catholics, Jews, and others who shared his opposition to abortion, homosexual behavior, and the liberal policies being enacted in Washington, D.C., at the time to join him in his effort to keep America from self-destructing. Some of his fellow fundamentalists immediately denounced him as a compromiser and began to speak out against his ministry.

Billy Graham faced the same problem when he began to invite Christian leaders from denominations some consider liberal or moderate to join him on the platform for his crusades. His critics didn't care that thousands of people might be saved during that crusade. They only cared that he was willing to work with people whose doctrine differed from theirs.

What do such attacks accomplish? The unchurched read about Christian leaders attacking one another and say what the young woman above said, "The world is negative enough without having the church make me more negative." Some read in the New Testament what it says about grace and wonder why such grace cannot be found in the church.

What Does the Bible Say About Grace?

Most Evangelical Christians readily admit that one enters into a relationship with God through Jesus Christ and that such a relationship cannot occur because of anything we do (see Rom. 3:20). It is strictly because of the grace of God that we can have our sins forgiven and experience adoption into the family of God (see 5:6-21). If we enter into the Christian life because of the grace of God, why do we then believe that our walk with God can only be perfected by our works? (See Gal. 3:2-3.) The apostle Paul goes so far as to say that "if righteousness comes through the law, then Christ died in vain" (2:21). Those are strong words, but true.

Paul goes on to write, "But if you bite and devour one another, beware lest you be consumed by one another!" (5:15). This is exactly what is happening today. When Christians attack one another because of music tastes, makeup, hair length, what versions of the Bible to use, and other foolishness, they end up destroying one another and their opportunities to witness to unbelievers. God cannot and will not use a graceless church. This is one of the problems the Pharisees had at the time of Jesus, and it still persists in many churches.

The thing I notice about modern-day Pharisees is that they are most critical of the sins they personally do not commit. It is easy for most Christians to attack homosexual and adulterous behavior because they do not struggle with those sins in their lives. However, the same passages in the Bible that list these as sins also include the sins of outbursts of anger, dissension, envy, and jealousy (see 1 Cor. 6:9-10; Gal. 5:19-21). How often do you hear today's Pharisees cry out against these sins? God must think they are important to include them with the others, but we tend to overlook these sins because these are the ones we all struggle to control.

Somewhere I heard a story about the pastor of a small community walking down the street when he met the town drunk. As they were walking and talking together, a group of small boys began throwing rocks at the drunk and calling him names. Turning to the pastor, the drunk said, "You see how these children treat me? Every time they see me on the street they throw rocks at me and call me names." The pastor smiled and said, "Maybe they are just trying to encourage you to straighten your life out." The drunk answered, "Maybe so, but I never read where Jesus ever threw rocks at anyone to help them do better." How true, and in fact, Jesus had some very strong words for the religious leaders who did want to throw rocks at a sinner. He said, "He who is without sin among you, let him throw a stone at her first" (John 8:7). With those words, everyone walked away without throwing a single stone. How much better would the church be if each of us followed this teaching?

In Matthew 7:5 Jesus had further words for those who are quick to judge the actions of others. He said, "Hypocrite! First remove the plank from your own eye, and then you will see clearly to remove the speck from your brother's eye." Let's be honest for a moment. Getting our own lives in order is a full-time job for each of us. None of us are absolutely perfect. If we would focus on correcting our own faults, we would be humble and gentler with everyone else around us. Self-righteousness and judgmental attitudes have no place in the Christian life. They are the enemies of grace.

I can tell you from firsthand experience that Jesus' teaching works. As I mentioned earlier, I used to drink alcohol. When I was first saved I continued to drink it. I enjoyed relaxing in the evening with a mixed drink. I did not drink to excess nor was I drinking in public, and I did not feel that I was harming anyone. Some Christian friends who helped lead me to Christ knew I continued to drink a little, but no one said a word about it even though they did not approve. One day at work I decided that I did not want to drink alcohol anymore, and when I went home I walked straight to the cabinet and poured every bottle of alcohol I had down the sink. I've never touched liquor since.

What would have happened if my friends had begun to chastise me for drinking? Knowing my personality, it would have probably caused me to be defensive and might have had a negative impact on our relationship. They simply let the Lord handle it. He is the one who helps us mature in our faith, and he doesn't need our help. Every person has to grow at a rate that is right for him or her, and if we try to interfere and speed up that process, we may do more harm than good. Every person in a church will be at a different level of spiritual maturity, and this is even more reason to extend grace to one another.

Isn't Grace Risky?

Yes it is, because once someone begins to emphasize grace, there will be some who will want to take advantage of it. There will always be those who will want to turn grace into license. Even the first-century church had to address this issue. The apostle Paul wrote, "What then? Shall we sin because we are not under law but under grace? Certainly not!" (Rom. 6:15).

Grace is not the same thing as license. We are not free to ignore clear teachings of Scripture while proclaiming we are no longer under the Law but under grace. Charles Swindoll writes:

Such rationalization is freedom gone to seed, liberty without limits . . . which is nothing more than disobedience in another dress. Some may see it as amazing grace; I call it abusing grace. Those who do so not only live confused and get hurt, but they confuse and hurt others. And that's what the latter half of Romans 6 is about: being so determined to fly free that you abuse the very freedom you've been given. We are wise to think of grace as a privilege to be enjoyed and protected, not a license to please ourselves.[3]

Some Christians walk away from their marriage vows and claim that grace allows them to do so. I know of a minister who explained his pending divorce from his wife of many years by saying that he had found someone else who made him much happier, and he knew that God wanted him to be happy. Such an attitude cheapens grace. We are to walk in the light we have been given (see Eph. 5:8). It is one thing to stumble and fail; it is something else entirely to willfully violate biblical teachings trusting that God will forgive us. Such presumption is dangerous and does not lead to spiritual growth.

Grace is also risky because it can so easily be misunderstood. Some preachers avoid preaching much about grace because they don't want to be accused of being soft on sin. I run the risk of being misunderstood for even writing this chapter for the same reason. The church needs to understand there is a difference between cheap grace and true grace. "'Cheap grace' justifies the *sin* rather than the sinner. True grace, on the other hand, justifies the *sinner,* not the sin."[4] We do not need to be afraid of true grace.

A Biblical Example

In 1 Corinthians, Paul addressed several issues in the Corinthian church. Chapter 5 contains his instructions regarding a church member who was living in open sin. Most Bible scholars believe this man was living in a sexual relationship with his stepmother. The church had done nothing about this activity, and in fact was demonstrating a great deal of tolerance toward it. No doubt they believed they were showing grace to this couple. Paul's command was simple: remove him from the church. Some readers will object at this point and ask, how is this an act of grace? Remember, cheap grace justifies the sin, and there was no way this sin could be justified. The man and his stepmother were unrepentant and obviously unwilling to change their lifestyle. The church had to confront such behavior for two reasons. One, this lifestyle would spiritually destroy both the man and his stepmother. The second reason is that such sin in the church can only lead to its own downfall. Sin is infectious and can spread rapidly. It must be addressed.

So where does grace come into play in this story? Grace is found in the motive behind Paul's strong words. This man was not to be removed from the church in order to banish him forever, but in the hope that it would help restore him. As long as the church continued to look the other way and not confront this blatant sin, the man and his lover would continue to live in their sin, perhaps even feeling that God approved of their arrangement. If the church exercised discipline and removed him from their fellowship, then it was possible that he could be convicted of his sin so that "his spirit may be saved in the day of the Lord Jesus" (1 Cor. 5:5). This call to discipline was not for final judgment but for restoration. Before Paul's letter, the church was exercising cheap grace toward this situation. Paul wanted them to provide true grace that would condemn the sin and restore the sinner to God. One commentator has correctly remarked, "To love the church and an individual enough to do what Paul suggested takes courage, deep confidence in God, and a mature love for people."[5]

Did Paul's recommendation work? Frankly, we don't know. Some scholars believe that Paul was referring to this man in 2 Corinthians 2:6-8. In that letter, Paul told the church that the man had repented and should be permitted to return to the fellowship. Evidently the church continued to punish and exclude this man even after he repented of his sin. They needed to reaffirm their love for him and return him to the church family.

The God of Second Chances

The apostle John wrote, "If we confess our sins, He is faithful and just to forgive us our sins and to cleanse us from all unrighteousness. If we say that we have not sinned, we make Him a liar, and His word is not in us. My little children, these things I write to you, so that you may not sin. And if anyone sins, we have an Advocate with the Father, Jesus Christ the righteous" (1 John 1:9—2:1).

All of us need God's grace. Any victory we experience over sin is due to that grace. Therefore, we do not have grounds to be judgmental toward others for their mistakes. The same grace that is available for the forgiveness of our sins and transforming our hearts is available to all people. You and I are the recipients of God's grace every single day, and we should not hesitate to extend grace to others.

Let's briefly look at two biblical examples of God offering second chances through his grace. Moses was raised in the court of Pharaoh. He was to be the means to deliver the Israelites from Egyptian slavery, but he acted rashly and murdered an Egyptian who was mistreating an Israelite slave and had to flee into the wilderness to save his own life. For forty years he worked as a shepherd in the wilderness until one day he came upon a burning bush. God spoke to him out of that bush and gave him the opportunity to fulfill his destiny and lead the Israelites to freedom. God had not washed his hands of Moses, but elevated him to a place of leadership and responsibility. Only God's grace could allow that to happen.

Centuries later, Jesus was about to be arrested. His disciples all swore they would stand with him, and as usual, Peter was the most vocal. He insisted he would lay his life down for Jesus' sake, but later that night he denied even knowing Jesus. Not once, but three times he swore he did not know the man. Soon after his third denial he came face-to-face with Jesus and went out and wept bitter tears. In Peter's mind he had blown it and there could be no restoration. He had his chance to take a stand for Jesus, but his fear of what might happen to him caused him to fail miserably. He had denied the Lord, and there was nothing left to do but return to his fishing boat. However, he soon learned that, like Moses, God wasn't done with him. After the resurrection Jesus met Peter and offered him forgiveness and restoration. Peter became another recipient of God's amazing grace.

There are some in the church today who would have written off both Moses and Peter, but God didn't. If a holy and just God can offer grace to men who failed him, why is it so hard for us—who have fallen more times than any of us would like to admit—to do the same? Has God called the church to sit as modern-day Pharisees—harshly and hypocritically judging one another—or has he called us to be channels of his grace? Each of us will have to make that determination for ourselves, but personally I want to be a channel of grace. I can only imagine where I would be today if not for the grace of God, and it would not be a good place. I have received so much of God's grace in my life; how could I do anything but offer it to others?

Summary

In many churches today, the grace of God is often preached about more than demonstrated. Too many in the church are grace-killers, not grace-givers. We Christians receive grace from God. As the recipients of God's grace, we are expected to extend that same grace to others. We must never make the mistake of thinking the church is simply a hotel for saints when, in reality, it is a hospital for sinners. At one time or another we will all need forgiveness and grace from one another. Let us all be quick to give that grace too, thereby helping one another on our journey through this life.

3

A Jack of Mission

The mission of the New Testament church is more about God's mission to the hurting, broken, lame, and lost than about institutional maintenance or pastoral care; but many church leaders have lost sight of this Great Commission and Great Commandment.[1]

—Edward Hammett

WHAT IS THE MISSION of your church? Now, I know what the politically correct answer is, but what is honestly the mission of your church? Wait a minute before you answer. After you think of your answer, look at your church calendar and your financial statement because it is in your calendar and your checkbook that we find the real mission of a church. Now tell me the mission of your church.

I am convinced that most churches I know really do not have a mission beyond providing services to their members. These churches have lost their heart for those who live in despair all around them. In fact, many of these churches no longer even see the people who live within the shadow of the church steeple. These churches are so inwardly focused that they cannot see those whose broken lives Jesus Christ came to save.

As a judicatory minister I have had the opportunity to work with many churches as they looked for new pastoral leadership. Consistently, these pastor search committees tell me the church wants a pastor who can grow their church, but trouble soon develops if their new pastor does begin to bring new people into the church. In too many churches these new people become a threat to the power base of existing members, and they take time and resources away from the existing members. Longtime church members begin to complain that the pastor is spending all his or her time reaching out to new people and neglecting the current members. As Reggie McNeal writes, "Member values clash with missionary values. Member values are all about church real estate, church programming, who's in and who's out, member services, member issues (translated: am I getting what I need out of this church?). Missionary values are about the street, people's needs, breaking down barriers, community issues (translated: am I partnering with God's work in people?)."[2]

McNeal believes that "the North American church is suffering from severe amnesia. It has forgotten why it exists."[3] The church is one of the few institutions in existence today that is supposed to exist for nonmembers as well as members. The church is called to make disciples, which involves both converting nonbelievers and nurturing believers. Neither group can be neglected. Both are called to continual growth in holiness. This goal conflicts with the self-centered, self-serving, and complacent attitudes present in so many congregations. Too many churches are neither concerned about going deeper with God nor reaching out to non-Christians. This lack of mission doesn't only strike big, country club-type churches. Even smaller churches can become so concerned about their continued existence that they refuse to do anything that might risk their limited resources. I tell churches all the time that I'm not sure God cares whether or not their church exists in the future; he is very concerned whether or not their church is on a mission with him in their communities. If a church will not be committed to mission and discipleship, God will leave that church to its own devices and raise up another church in that community that will. Here's a secret for any church that is concerned about whether or not it survives in the future: identify the mission God has for your church and pour everything you have into that mission. As long as a church is on a mission with God, he will never allow that church to die.

Why Would Anyone Want to Attend Your Church?

This is a question I frequently ask in my workshops for small church leaders. America is dotted with small churches, especially in the Midwest where I live. Most of these churches offer very similar programs and worship styles. Because of my work, I attend a different church almost every Sunday and I can go for weeks and never experience anything different, regardless of which church I attend. It's like we believe there is only one way to do church. Many of the people who attend do so because their families attended that particular church. Of course, that is quickly becoming less and less of a reason for someone to attend a church. Neither of our two children attends a church of the denomination in which they were raised, nor do they attend a church in which their spouse was raised. They have found their own churches that offer ministries that speak to their life needs. Both were newer churches when they began attending them, and these churches had a very clear focus for their ministries. They developed ministries that addressed the needs of the people in their community. It is worth noting that both grew large very quickly because of that focus.

Existing churches tend to offer a shotgun approach to ministry. They believe if they offer enough programs that they will surely appeal to someone. Megachurches can do that, but most of our churches cannot. For example, Thomas Road Baptist Church in Lynchburg, Virginia, offers fifteen different support groups each week, and in the spring and fall they offer around two hundred community groups that appeal to a host of different interests. This church also claims about twenty-four thousand members. They can afford to offer a broad variety of ministry opportunities to their community, and you can be certain that each one of them will be done with excellence.

How many different ministries could your church offer with excellence? What are the human and financial resources you have available to invest in ministry to your community? I doubt most church leaders reading this book would say they could compete with a megachurch and offer over two hundred ministry opportunities to their community each week. In fact, I doubt that most of your churches could offer more than four or five ministries, and for many of you it might be only one ministry. If you've sat down and determined that your church could only offer one specific ministry to your community that you could do with excellence, that is okay.

Be faithful in preaching the gospel, growing in grace, and loving others. This is your purpose for existing.

Why would anyone want to attend your church? The answer is because you offer a ministry through which God speaks to their deepest needs. You are providing an excellent ministry that really addresses the issues they have in their lives.

We Have Little Heart for Mission

There is nothing complicated about identifying the mission of a church. Jesus told us that mission when he gave us the Great Commission and the Great Commandment. The mission of every church is found in those two, small statements, and that mission has never changed. Let me ask you another question . . . when was the last time your church board spent much time discussing either one? Do you get bogged down in the details of maintenance without expressing a heart for your mission?

I discussed maintenance-minded churches at length in an earlier book[4] so I won't repeat myself here except to say that most smaller churches, and many larger ones too, prefer maintenance over mission. There's less risk, and no one ever has to learn anything new. Many pastors complain about this mentality in their churches, but the fact is that many pastors prefer serving in maintenance-minded churches. We'll talk about these pastors in the next chapter.

We must recapture the passion the early church had for the Great Commission and the Great Commandment. These must once again become the driving forces behind everything our churches do. Only then will we impact our communities for Jesus Christ as the early church did. Unfortunately, if we are honest we will admit that neither the Great Commission nor the Great Commandment drives many churches. It has been well said, "If only God's people would spend as much time and money learning how to be witnesses as they do reading a fiction series on the end times, then maybe we would not be living on the only continent in the world where the church is not growing."[5]

The church in Acts could not be stopped despite incredible persecution. Their leaders were beaten and their lives were threatened, but they would not be silenced. Countless numbers of Christians were martyred, but still the church grew. The more the persecution against them grew, the more the church spread until they became known as the people who turned the world upside down (see Acts 17:6).

When the church has been at its best it has had a heart to reach those whose sins have separated them from God. This passion is what compelled John Wesley to travel over two hundred thousand miles, mostly on horseback, to preach the gospel to every crowd he could gather. It is what led Moravian converts in Africa to sell themselves into slavery so they could take the gospel to other slaves in the new world. This same passion is what has enabled underground churches in China and other Communist nations to flourish and grow. It is this passion that leads men and women to start new churches and Bible studies in their homes, storefronts, and other locations, and it is this passion that the church must recapture if it is to ever again be used by God to transform lives.

Where Does This Passion Originate?

It begins by seeing humankind through the eyes of God. Romans 3:23 is very clear when it says "for all have sinned and fall short of the glory of God." "All" simply means every one of us—no one is excluded. Every person who has ever lived has been born with self-centeredness and rebellion in his or her heart. We have all sinned, and as Romans 6:23 tells us, "the wages of sin is death, but the gift of God is eternal life in Christ Jesus our Lord." If that isn't clear enough, John MacArthur Jr. explains, "Spiritual death is earned. It is the just and rightful compensation for a life that is characterized by sin, which is *every* life apart from God."[6]

As MacArthur said, Paul was talking about spiritual death. Obviously, everyone will die a physical death so that cannot be what he is referring to. The death that is caused by our fallen nature is spiritual death—separation from God. The Bible is clear that each of us has an eternal destination. Those who have trusted in Jesus Christ as their Lord and Savior will spend eternity with him in heaven. Those who rejected him in this lifetime will be eternally separated from him in hell. This is the second death that we read about in Revelation 20:11-15.

Now, I understand that people today do not find a discussion of hell to be politically correct. Even many church people prefer to not hear sermons about hell. In our pluralistic society, it simply isn't considered proper to talk about a loving God sending anyone to hell, and this is part of the reason we lack passion for the Great Commission in many of our churches today. We do not want to believe that God will allow anyone to spend eternity in a place of fire and torment, especially if this person is someone we have known and loved all our lives.

We also are no longer comfortable proclaiming that Jesus Christ is the only way to God. Surely, society thinks today, all of these other religions can't be wrong. For some reason they have no problem believing that Christians are wrong in their assertion that Jesus Christ is the only way to God, but they cannot believe that the other religions just might be the ones that have it wrong. Jesus said, "I am the way, the truth, and the life. No one comes to the Father except through Me" (John 14:6). Speaking of Jesus, the apostle Peter said, "Nor is there salvation in any other, for there is no other name under heaven given among men by which we must be saved" (Acts 4:12). The apostle Paul affirmed, "If you confess with your mouth the Lord Jesus and believe in your heart that God has raised Him from the dead, you will be saved" (Rom. 10:9).

To make these claims in the twenty-first century is considered improper and exclusivist. Postmodern man insists that we must accept all beliefs as equally true and legitimate. Those who make such arguments fail to realize that every religious system is exclusive and claims to have the truth.[7]

Seeing humankind through the eyes of God entails understanding our situation in light of Scripture. As I said before, everything you believe will depend on what you believe about the Bible. If you accept the Bible as authoritative, then you should have no trouble believing that humankind is separated from God because of the bent toward sin that exists in each of us and that the only way to have any kind of personal relationship with God is through Jesus Christ. If you do not accept the Bible as authoritative, you will not understand the true problem with humanity or the reason for God's solution to that problem, and you will not be passionate about evangelistic and discipleship ministry.

When we truly believe that man is separated from God apart from Jesus Christ and that hell is the eternal destiny of all who die in that condition, we will begin to see people through the eyes of God. It is said that if sinners could only get a glimpse of what hell is like, they would repent and turn to God. I believe that it is not only the sinners who need a glimpse of hell—so do Christians. If we who profess faith in Jesus Christ saw even for an instant the fate of all who die without Christ in their lives, the world would not be able to stop our efforts to tell everyone we know about the grace of God that gives life to all who will receive it. It would reignite a passion in us that much of the church has not felt in decades and would return the church to its true mission.

When a Church Recaptures Its Mission

"There is nothing more important related to fulfilling the
Great Commission than a church which understands that
this commission is central to its mission, has structured its
ministry around the centrality of this mission, has created an
environment that welcomes outsiders into this mission,
and deploys insiders in fulfilling this mission."[8]
—Ed Stetzer and David Putnam

When a church recaptures its mission, it structures everything around that mission. Maintenance-only ministry takes a backseat to fulfilling the Great Commission. The church no longer exists merely for the comfort and convenience of its members. It understands that God has commissioned it to lead Christians into the deeper life of faith and reach those who have not yet responded to the gospel, and it directs it resources to fulfill that mission.

Such a church is more than evangelistic; it becomes missional. In the past we have too often been satisfied with leading someone to Christ, and we have stopped there. Missional churches realize such a decision is only the first step a person will take. Missional churches are interested in transformation.

The church has also been pushing an agenda or program for growth, but missional churches are not primarily concerned with church growth in the traditional sense. Milfred Minatrea explains, "For missional churches, the goal of church growth is not to get bigger. The goal is to equip more people to live as authentic disciples of Jesus Christ. The measure has to do with function, not size."[9]

Missional churches move beyond their desire for survival and become risk-takers. They learn the culture of the area where they are located and find ways to relate to that culture. Maintenance-minded churches seek to repeat the same old ministries that used to be effective without ever stopping to consider the context in which they are now doing ministry. Missional churches seek to be relevant to their current context in order to transform it.

A church that recaptures its mission makes another significant change in understanding its purpose. It realizes that while it has a responsibility to support mission work around the world, its primary mission field is in its own backyard. A missional church understands that it is to be a missionary church in the culture in which is exists.[10] Members of a missional church will also begin to see themselves as missionaries to that culture. Such a church takes time to understand the needs that exist in its context and finds ways to minister to those needs. The missionaries that meet each week in the missional church do so in order to worship God and to be equipped to go out into their mission field to work for the kingdom of God. No longer are the worship services merely a "bless me" hour, but they become a training opportunity for believers to grow as disciples and as missionaries. Minatrea defines a missional church as "a reproducing community of authentic disciples, being equipped as missionaries sent by God, to live and proclaim His Kingdom in their world."[11] In the missional church this occurs in the worship services, small groups, and whenever God's people gather.

Recapturing the Mission Will Require Change

I question whether most churches really do not know what their mission should be. Sermons are regularly preached on the Great Commission and the Great Commandment. Go into any Christian bookstore and you will find numerous books explaining how churches can fulfill a mission centered around both of these. I believe that most churches understand what their mission should be, but they avoid committing themselves to it because it will require too many changes in what they are currently doing.

Most people find change very unsettling. So much of life today is changing. It is nice to be able to go to church each Sunday and find one thing in our lives that has not changed much in decades. We may replace the hymnals from time to time, but the new ones have mostly the same old hymns, and we seldom learn the newer songs. We prefer to sing the ones we've sung for years. We sit in the same pew Sunday after Sunday. Some people sit in the same places their parents and grandparents sat. We expect our pastors to do the same ministries that their predecessors did, and most of those ministries are primarily centered around caring for the existing flock. We seldom start new Sunday school classes because we don't want to do anything to disrupt the fellowship we enjoy in our current classes, even though we know that existing classes seldom attract new people after they have existed for more than eighteen months.[12]

If we took seriously the fact that fulfilling the Great Commission and the Great Commandment is the mission of our church, we would have to be willing to risk changing all these things and even more. If we found that the racial and ethnic population of our surrounding neighborhood had changed, we might have to find ways to minister to people who are different from us. Even if the racial and ethnic population has not changed, that does not mean the neighborhood hasn't changed. There could be persons of a different economic status living in our communities. We might find there are large numbers of single-parent homes. We might find there are large numbers of people struggling with various addictions. We may find a larger population of homosexuals than we ever imagined. How could our church minister to these different needs? The answer is that we can't unless we are willing to change how we do ministry. If we continue to plug along as we have since the fifties, we will be unable to minister to anyone different from us. But, if we are willing to minister as missionaries, we will find ways to minister to the society around us.

This will require a huge paradigm shift in how many of our churches do ministry, and personally I am not convinced that some of our churches will be able to make that shift. They will be unwilling to make the changes that are required. Some of those churches are in such a state of decline that they cannot make such changes, but most of those unwilling to do so refuse because they lack compassion for those who do not have a relationship with Jesus Christ. They either don't truly believe that the lost face an eternity separated from God, or they simply don't care enough to change in order to reach as many people as possible. Either reason reflects a serious heart condition in these churches.

Legacy Churches

This may be the most challenging section in the entire book. I first heard of legacy churches from a book written by Stephen Gray and Franklin Dumond.[13] Both of these men are denominational leaders in the General Association of General Baptists and Senior Consultants with New Church Specialties. They have over fifty years of ministerial experience between them. A legacy church is one that realizes it is poor stewardship to spend all of its resources on life support. Instead, a legacy church gives its assets to another ministry that is more effectively reaching people for the kingdom of God.

Every year approximately five thousand churches in America close their doors. Unfortunately, many of these churches had died years earlier. Because of the past faithfulness of previous members, they had the resources to continue to open their doors each week, but there had been no ministry in many of these churches for years (perhaps decades). Every year they dipped into their reserves to cover the budget shortfalls. They reduced their expenses to the bare minimum in order to make their resources last as long as possible. Once those resources dried up, they had no choice but to close their doors. How much better would it have been if years earlier they had been willing to admit that their ministry was over and they turned their assets over to their denomination or another church for the express purpose of starting a new church rather than spend away all their financial assets on life support?

Gray and Dumond explain that "churches bent on 'survival at any cost' are interested in building their own empire. Churches bent on building the kingdom of God look beyond their own survival to the greater work of spreading the good news of Christ."[14] Unfortunately, we have the mistaken belief that a church is established to last forever, and many Christians believe that if a church closes, it represents a failure for the kingdom of God. If that is true, then every church written about in Acts was a failure because none of those churches exist today.[15] It is entirely possible for a church to come into existence to meet a current need and then close when that need no longer exists so that another one can be born that will meet the new needs.

I wrote earlier about the large number of smaller churches in the Midwest where I live. Why are there so many churches? When most of these churches came into existence, people either walked or rode horses or buggies to church. Every small community needed their own church because even though the next community might only be five or ten miles away, it would take too long for people to get to church. That is hardly the case today. Many of these small communities were once vibrant towns, but today barely exist. Their schools were consolidated into county-wide schools decades ago. Stores and gas stations closed. Many of these communities are simply a speed limit sign on a highway that few people travel. But, their churches continue to be open for a handful of faithful people who have long ago forgotten the original purpose for which the church was established. These are often sweet, God-fearing people who believe it is their duty to keep their little church open, despite the fact that there is little ministry and little purpose in the church remaining open.

They really do not understand why new people are not attracted to their church and live with the fear that their church may have to close in their lifetime.

Sometimes these dying churches are not in small, rural communities but are found in growing population areas. Perhaps their communities have changed and the church refused to change with them. Several years ago I had a telephone interview with a pastor search committee who told me that almost all of their members came from three areas of their city, none of which were around their church. They admitted that almost no one from the immediate community attended their church. The church was located only a couple of hours from my home, so one afternoon my wife and I decided to see if we could find it. It didn't take me long to recognize that the community around the church was much different racially and economically than the persons who attended the church. The current membership had moved to new suburban communities when new people began to move into the neighborhood. Although the church members are willing to drive in for church services each week, that church will remain in a state of decline until they decide to reach out to their new community. At the time I spoke with the committee, it became clear that they were not interested in any intentional outreach to their new neighbors. Such churches would be better off as legacy churches and give their assets to a ministry that will effectively reach the new community.

There are many examples of legacy churches. The Evangelical Covenant Church in Poway, California, closed its doors in 1995. Its assets were used to plant twenty-five new churches that have an attendance of over ten thousand people.[16]

The Metropolitan Church in Kansas City, Kansas, once boasted of a congregation of over 350 people. However, their community began to change, and in time, their congregation had shrunk to a fraction of what it once was. A new church, Risen Lamb, was started to reach the community and soon outgrew its facilities. The congregation of Metropolitan Church voted to give its $1,500,000 property to Risen Lamb in order to best reach the community. This brave congregation was willing to give up its shared history and traditions in order to allow the kingdom of God to advance.[17]

What these and other legacy churches have in common is a love for the kingdom of God. They realize it isn't about their continued existence as a church; it's about advancing the kingdom and seeing people's lives transformed by the power of God. These churches have a heart for ministry and are willing to do whatever it takes for ministry to occur. To decide to become a legacy church is one of the most unselfish things a church can do.

Summary

Churches are either focused on maintenance or mission, and unfortunately too many of our churches today have lost their sense of mission. Their ministries are all about keeping their current membership comfortable. We simply must recapture the urgency that is behind the Great Commission and the Great Commandment. These were not suggestions our Lord gave us; they are the marching orders for the church. Any church that refuses to be about mission will find itself replaced by a new church that will reach out to those for whom Jesus Christ gave his life.

To become a church on mission will require extensive change for many congregations. We will have to be willing to give up some of our cherished programs and preferences in order to minister in a way that will transform people in our postmodern society. Mission will have to become the driving force behind everything we do, and anything that does not contribute to that mission will have to be abandoned.

Some churches will not be able to make these changes, and many others will refuse to do so. Such churches are either no longer able to see people through the eyes of God, or they do not really believe that people need God in their lives. Neither reason is acceptable. Perhaps the question that we must be asking ourselves is, do we really love people as God does?

For those churches unable to make the changes necessary to become a church on mission, perhaps the best thing they could do is to become a legacy church, donating their resources to new churches that can impact their communities for Christ. Churches that have little chance of regaining a vital ministry will find this to be the most unselfish thing they could do for God's kingdom.

4
A Lack of Pastoral Leadership

---

*We have observed that the biggest human factor
in the process of transforming a dysfunctional
congregation to a healthy one is the
leadership ability of the pastor.*[1]

—Paul Borden

CHURCHES ARE OFTEN quite happy with the status quo. Many of them complain about a lack of growth, but a large percentage of them do not mean it. In fact, if a new pastor came and tried to introduce the kinds of changes required for the church to grow, the congregation would be quick to declare that his or her first obligation is to them. Pastor search committees often mislead potential candidates about what the church wants. This is not usually intentional; it's just that everybody is saying the correct things about wanting the church to grow and to reach new people for Christ, but many of them do not recognize what they are saying.

When churches say they desire a transformational leader, they usually have no idea what they're really asking for. Often they mean someone who will bring just enough change to keep the pews and offering plates full. Pastors have historically been rewarded for being effective managers, for keeping the church stable and moving. Pastors who are transformational leaders often find they are not universally valued or praised.[2]

A large number of these churches do not want to call a pastor who is a transformational leader. They want a chaplain, a manager, a shepherd, and that is fine with most pastors because they haven't been trained to be leaders anyway. Most seminaries teach pastors how to manage an organization, how to exegete Scripture, how to counsel, but they do not teach how to lead. Many do not even offer an elective class on leadership. As a result, students graduate from seminary with a lot of knowledge but no real idea of how to provide leadership to a church. If Borden's statement above is correct, and I believe it is, the first few churches this new pastor serves will not receive the leadership they need to be as effective for the kingdom of God as they could be.

Defining Leadership

Leadership is one of those words that is used a lot today but seldom defined. Before a person can evaluate his or her own leadership abilities, it is necessary to define what is meant by leadership.

Some define leadership as influence. If no one is following, then the person is not a leader. There is some truth in this, but there is more to the kind of leadership churches need. After all, people may follow someone in the wrong direction. Jim Jones was a leader, but he led people to their deaths. Others equate leadership with position. They believe since they are in positions of leadership, such as senior pastor, then they must be leaders. Leadership has nothing to do with position. Very seldom, except in the largest churches, is a new pastor a leader in his or her church during the first few years of service. Someone else whom the church trusts is the real leader.

If none of these adequately define leadership, then how can it be defined? Out of the many I've seen, I identify best with George Barna's definition: "Leadership is the process of motivating, mobilizing, resourcing, and directing people to passionately and strategically pursue a vision from God that a group jointly embraces."[3] Barna's definition of leadership begins with having a vision, which I believe is essential to the success and health of any organization, and leading others in the pursuit of that vision. Not only is the leader leading followers, he or she is leading them in the right direction: the fulfillment of God's vision for their church.

Now that we have a definition of leadership, we can ask how many pastors are providing this kind of leadership. Repeatedly, we are told that 80 percent of the churches in North America have plateaued or are declining. While many pastors would claim they are leading their churches, where is the fruit of that leadership? They may be excellent managers, which is what they were trained to do, but few of the pastors of these plateaued and declining churches are providing the kind of leadership that could turn their churches around. In fact, in many of these churches the pastors will not stay there long enough to ever provide leadership to the church.

A long-term pastorate is no guarantee that a church will be healthy and enjoy a productive ministry, but a plateaued church will never turn around without a long-term commitment from its pastor. Change does not come easy to churches, and change will be required if a church is to turn itself around. After all, if a church simply continues to do what it has been doing, it will remain in the same condition it is in. The only way to help a church break out of bad habits is to introduce change, and it takes a trusted leader to do that. That trust is only given to such a leader when he or she has been there long enough to earn it.

Why Do More Pastors Not Lead?

The first reason pastors don't lead has already been mentioned: many of them have never been trained to lead. They attend seminary to prepare for ministry, but too many seminaries fail to teach leadership principles to their students. The typical master of divinity degree will consist of ninety or more hours of study but may never include even a single class on leadership. Pastors tell me they never had a class that addressed strategic planning, financial management, relationship building, or even how to conduct a church business meeting. A running joke among ministers is that it takes them seven to ten years to get over their seminary training before they can become effective ministers. It would be funny if it wasn't so true and so unfair to both the ministers and the churches they serve.

I am not against seminary training. In fact, I have two seminary degrees, but I refused to go with the traditional master of divinity degree. I earned a master of arts in religion with a concentration in leadership and a doctor of ministry in which I took a number of leadership courses. The master of divinity focuses much of its required course work in disciplines that would be great for the student wanting to pursue a PhD and teach in a university or seminary, but that is not what most seminary students plan to do when they graduate. Most will be serving in a local church as a pastor or staff person. For many pastors, a master of arts may provide the balance of theological and practical studies that would be better suited for pastoral ministry.

The master of divinity became the standard degree for pastors when denominations sought to make the pastorate more professional. Some denominations have determined that this degree is the minimum educational requirement for ordination, and those clergy who have not earned this degree are often given second-class status.[4] I serve in one of those denominations, and my ordination is looked upon by some as less than fully recognized. However, in many conservative churches, these pastors can find a home because these churches are often more concerned that their pastor has a call from God to the ministry and that he or she is competent than that the pastor has a particular degree.[5]

My proposal is that seminaries and denominations get together and determine what pastors need to know to successfully lead their churches in the twenty-first century and develop degree programs based on that. The seminaries should continue to offer the master of divinity for those students planning to pursue even more advanced theological degrees, such as the master of theology, the doctor of theology, or the doctor of philosophy and minister within an academic setting. For the majority of students who are planning to serve in local churches, they should be offered master of arts, master of arts in religion, master of Christian education, and similar degrees designed to help them provide the kind of leadership their churches need to be transformed. Such degrees can include sufficient classes in theology and the Bible to ensure that these students are theologically sound in their teaching.

Churches Won't Let Their Pastors Lead

A second reason that more pastors do not lead their churches is that their churches do not allow it. Any attempt by the pastor to provide leadership would be met with immediate resistance. A pastor told me that the church he recently went to revised their constitution during the pastor search process and virtually stripped all authority from the pastor and placed it within the lay leadership. Of course, they did not tell him this during the interview process. His basic duties now consist of preaching and overseeing the various ministries of the church, but he has no authority over those ministries. This is a church that averages several hundred people on Sunday mornings and needs strong pastoral leadership, but controlling lay leaders in the church have made it impossible for the pastor to provide such leadership.

These churches all say the right things. They say they want a pastor who will grow their church. They say they want to reach out and impact their communities. They say they want to make a difference in the kingdom of God. They tell the pastor, especially when they are calling a new pastor, that they want him or her to lead them and move the church forward, but when he or she attempts to do so, they immediately press the brakes to make sure the church can't go forward. When the church doesn't grow as the congregation wishes, guess who gets blamed? A church cannot hold a pastor responsible for the health or growth of the church when it refuses to give him or her the authority to lead the church. You cannot assign responsibility if you haven't given authority.

There are many reasons why a church will not allow the pastor to lead. Some churches have a strong, core group of "controllers" who will block any change they perceive as a threat to their power. I addressed controllers in an earlier book,[6] so I will only mention here that in some churches as much as 20 percent of the congregation may be made up of controllers. Typically, 60 percent of the church doesn't want any trouble, so if the controllers oppose the pastor's attempts to introduce change, they will also oppose it to maintain the peace. A pastor in such a situation should know that it might take years to change this environment, and it may be so entrenched that it will never change until these controllers leave the church. I know that's not very nice to say, but unfortunately it is true.

I recently heard of a new pastor who attended his first deacon meeting. In that meeting he asked the deacons who were the people in the church he needed to watch. One of the deacons immediately responded, "You're talking to them." That pastor was in trouble before his ministry in that church ever started. Most controllers are not bold enough to announce their presence, and it showed how entrenched they were.

Controllers should not be allowed to limit the impact of a church on their community. The only reason they continue to negatively influence the ministry of the church is because the remainder of the church does not have the courage to stand up to them. As one pastor said to me, "The problem in our church is that we are made up of nice people who do not want to take on the handful that are not so nice." The same could be said of many churches. We give a handful of people veto power over any effort to move the church forward into ministry. Regardless of what we say we want to see happen in our churches, it will never happen as long as the congregation is more concerned about not offending the controllers than about reaching people with the gospel of Christ. This reflects a spine problem. Such churches need to grow a spine and confront these controllers once and for all. Tom Bandy challenges churches to ask themselves if they love the controllers in their churches more than they do their own teenagers and others who have not been reached with the gospel. It is an important question.[7]

We must begin seeing controllers as cancers in the church. They are the unhealthy cells that destroy healthy cells in the body. If a cancer is not stopped, it can end the life of the body. The earlier it is stopped, the greater the potential for a long, healthy life. When doctors diagnose most cancers, they recommend immediate and strong procedures. Radiation, chemotherapy, and even surgery are often necessary to ensure that the cancer is completely removed from the body. These treatments are not easy for the person to go through, but it is only when the cancer is removed that the body regains its health. Challenging the controllers will normally be painful, but until their influence is eliminated, the church will never be healthy and able to function as God intends.

One final point about dealing with controllers—this is not a battle the pastor can win alone. In fact, many pastors who take on the controllers end up unemployed. This is a battle that the congregation must decide to fight. Pastors must be wary of the congregation too. Often a pastor will be encouraged to take on the controllers only to find that when the going gets tough, the congregation is nowhere to be seen. Roy Oswald recognizes the danger in this: "Clergy should watch out for the trap set when members complain to them about the patriarch or matriarch of the parish and encourage the pastor to take the parental figure on. Clergy who respond to such mutinous bids, expecting the congregation to back them in the showdown, betray their misunderstanding of the dynamics of small-church ministry."[8]

Although Oswald was speaking here of smaller churches, the same dynamic is true in larger ones as well. This is a battle the congregation will have to fight if it is to be won. The pastor can best lead from the rear by giving encouragement and praying for those in the heat of the battle. There are times when the congregation must decide for themselves what kind of church they are going to be, and this is one of those times.

During my pastorate there was a situation that created a lot of turmoil in the church. A handful of members were upset over a salary increase the finance committee had recommended for me. I imagine the telephone lines around our rural church were cherry red at times as they continued calling people to complain about this decision and try to get people to oppose it. Perhaps to their surprise they encountered a lot of opposition to their opposition! There were some very strong arguments between members. I was accused by some of manipulating the finance committee so they would recommend the salary increase, but quite honestly, I was as surprised as anyone when they told me their recommendation.

One thing I knew was that although this battle was being fought over my salary, it really wasn't about me. The old guard and the newer leaders who had come into the church were locked in a battle to decide what kind of church they were going to be in the future. I believed that my involvement in this disagreement would only create future problems. The church was at a crossroads, and the members had to decide for themselves what kind of church they wanted. I contacted our judicatory leader, and he agreed with my assessment. He met with the opposing parties and felt even stronger that my perspective was right. During the next business meeting, I left the room when the budget for the new year was presented. For an hour I sat in my study and listened to angry voices coming from the meeting room. Finally, a vote was taken and I was asked to return. The budget passed with my salary increase intact.

The ones who opposed it were not happy, but the church benefited in many ways from this battle. We had weathered a major storm and survived. New leaders demonstrated they would stand up to the older leaders if they believed their position was the right one. They decided what the church would look like in the future, and I had not been caught in the middle. Finally, the negative things the controllers claimed would happen did not happen. My salary increase did not cause us to lose members, and our offerings actually increased rather than deceased. Our church became much stronger because of the way this disagreement was handled.

Another reason some churches refuse to allow the pastor to lead is that they have been burnt by pastors in the past. Let's admit it, there are some very unhealthy people out there serving as pastors. Some are arrogant, controlling, and unwilling to listen to anyone's counsel.

A judicatory leader recently told me about one of his churches that had left the denomination to join another one. They had a new pastor, and within two months he convinced the church to make the change. Although this was the pastor's first church, the judicatory leader said that he is one of the most arrogant people he has ever met. Still in seminary, he seems convinced that he knows all truth, and anyone who challenges anything he says or does immediately becomes the enemy. Supposedly, he has already told the church that things will be done his way or he will leave. It is amazing to me that a church would abandon a 150-year history with a denomination because of the wishes of a person they have known for two months. Already, this judicatory leader is hearing rumblings that people are not happy with this pastor's leadership, but so far no one has had the courage to challenge him.

Such authoritarian leaders are toxic to the church.[9] If they are not challenged, the church may never recover, and if they are challenged or removed, the church will likely be very cautious about their future pastors. In the interest of preventing toxic leaders from creating problems in the future, lay leaders may simply not allow future pastors to lead.

Dictatorial leaders need to be removed from our churches and replaced by true servant leaders. Stephen Covey defines a servant leader as "one who seeks to draw out, inspire, and develop the best and highest within people from the inside out."[10] He or she does this by helping the church identify God's vision for them, then leading the church to fulfill that vision. Each person is challenged and invited to use his or her gifts and passions in this work. The servant leader goes out ahead to identify the obstacles that might prevent the vision from being fulfilled and works with the congregation to remove those barriers. He or she provides the resources and encouragement that enable the vision to be fulfilled. The servant leader takes Ephesians 4:11-12 seriously and equips all the members of the church to minister so that God's purposes might be realized.

Servant leaders do not force a congregation to adopt a particular vision for the church, nor do they have a "my way or the highway" attitude. They do not beat people down for disagreeing with them on political, denominational, or even theological issues. When differences occur, they enter into dialogue and try to work through their differences. Sometimes those differences are great and cannot be resolved. When that is the case, servant leaders realize they are not a good fit for that place of ministry and move on to one that is a better fit. Always, in spite of the differences, there is respect for others.

When churches have not been served by true servant leaders they may distrust future pastors. It is important for a pastor to learn the history of previous pastors and the relationship that existed between the church and those pastors. It is critically important to find out if a previous pastor had been terminated or asked to resign. If this has happened with a number of former pastors, it will be an indication that this church has not had a healthy relationship with their pastors and is unlikely to entrust leadership to future pastors.

The last reason churches will not allow their pastors to lead is that they are content with the status quo. Over the years, churches often unknowingly develop systems that determine how large they will become. In my workshops I frequently tell leaders their churches are exactly the size they want them to be. Sometimes a church will protest that they want to be larger, and I respond if they really did, they would be growing. Every county in the United States is a rich minefield of unchurched persons, and some counties have more than 80 percent of their population not involved in any church. The fields are certainly white with harvest, so why don't more churches reach the unchurched population? It's because they don't want to make the changes that are required to reach the current generation growing up without God. These churches are apathetic about the spiritual needs of their unchurched neighbors and content to enjoy the status quo.

These maintenance-minded churches seek pastors who can keep the church machinery running smoothly. For them, success means paying their budget each year, receiving regular visits from the pastor in their homes or hospital rooms, having a sufficient number of pitch-in, or potluck, dinners for fellowship, and an absence of conflict. If a few of the church members' children are baptized each year, that is considered to be an excellent year of evangelism.

Such churches seldom see the needs that exist outside their building, or if they do, they wonder why someone doesn't do something about them, and by "someone" they mean someone *else*. These churches often insist they are mission-minded because they send a few dollars each year to their denominational mission organization, but they don't realize that they are neglecting the mission field outside their doors.

Such churches just want to be left alone to gather each Sunday and sing their familiar hymns with people who are also familiar to them. Their pastor is expected to preach each week and provide a level of pastoral care that will satisfy their needs. Anything beyond that is discouraged. These churches see the outside world as a hostile place, and they want to gather in their holy huddle to protect themselves from the dangers that exist out there. To change their traditional ways of doing things in an effort to reach new people is seen as compromising with the world. Such churches are locked in a fifties mind-set, and they love it. It's all they know, and it's all they want to know. Any effort to change such churches is highly unlikely to succeed. Unfortunately, the best thing to do with such churches is to leave them alone until their doors finally close.

Some Pastors Don't Want to Lead

A third reason why some pastors don't lead their churches is that they don't want to. Not only have they not been trained how to lead a church, but they have no desire for a leadership role. Many pastors do not see themselves as leaders. They do not believe they have leadership gifts, and they do not think they are called to lead.[11] Such pastors often define the role of a pastor by the models of ministry they saw growing up. I grew up in a time when pastors prepared sermons, visited in the homes and hospital rooms of their members, and presented a proper role model to the community. They were not involved in political issues and seldom involved in any controversies unless one developed within the church. They seldom tried to introduce change into the church but simply maintained what had always been done in that particular church. That was the model I took with me to my pastorate, and it was the model I followed for many years. This is a perfect fit for churches that do not want to upset the status quo.

Many pastors have been taught how to manage a local church; the church rewards them for their management skills, not their leadership skills, and they have no interest in trying to lead their churches into new areas of ministry. Someone recently told me that a seminary education will prepare a person to pastor a church of 120, but if a pastor wants to lead a larger church, he or she will have to learn new skills. That probably explains why the typical North American church runs about 75 people on Sunday morning and why few single-pastor churches seldom have more than 120 people on a normal Sunday morning.

Of course, some pastors are not interested in leading their church because of the frustrations that are a part of the job. Many are woefully underpaid, which puts financial pressure on their families. In some churches pastors spend all their time addressing one conflict after another. It is not uncommon for churches to make so many demands on their pastors that those pastors don't have time to lead even if they wanted to. Such pastors struggle to find time for their families and their own self-care, and the last thing they want is to add a new ministry to their already-overloaded plates.

Many pastors do not want to lead their churches because they don't know where they are going. John Maxwell tells us that "all leaders have two common characteristics: first, they are going somewhere; second, they are able to persuade other people to go with them."[12] Notice the order in his statement. First, the leaders know where they are going. If the leader isn't going anywhere, he or she will be unable to ask anyone to join the journey. Too many pastors simply are not going anywhere. They are mired in the ministry ruts they or their churches have created. Like the Israelites, they keep wandering in the wilderness, hoping that someday something good will happen in their ministries or in the church, but they have no idea how to help make it happen.

Pastors frequently admit they have no vision for their ministries. They don't know what to do and don't know how to discover what they need to do. What is even more bothersome is that after admitting their lack of vision for ministry, they do nothing to try to discern God's vision for their future. You can talk to them a year or two later and they still don't have any sense of vision. By that time, they are usually ready to move on to another church and one has to wonder how many of those moves are done in hopes of finding some purpose for one's life and ministry.

Discerning God's vision for one's life and church is hard work, and many pastors are not willing to put in the time and effort to do it. However, without such vision, the pastor and the church cannot expect long-term success in ministry. Vision gives direction and purpose and instills a passion in both the pastor and the church that can lead to a fruitful ministry. Mike Regele flatly states,

We need leaders who are driven by moral vision . . . A visionary leader is a leader who is driven by a clear image of an ideal condition, a condition that does not satisfactorily exist. It is a vision of what ought to be in the lives of people, in contrast to what is . . . The disparity between "what is" and "what ought to be" generates passion in the heart of the leader. A passion in the soul compels him or her to transform this vision into reality. Such passion has a distinctly moral quality to it.[13]

Christian psychologist Gary Collins insists that one cannot be a leader if he or she lacks vision. "If you think you can be a leader without being a visionary, forget it. No one will follow your lead if you don't know where you're going. If you want to be successful in your work, raise your kids effectively, be a good teacher, grow a church, or build a business, you better have a vision."[14]

I do not know why many pastors seem so uninterested in seeking God's vision for their churches. It seems logical that knowing God's purpose for one's church would enable the pastor and church to minister more effectively. Decisions would be simplified. If a proposed plan of action fit within the vision, it would receive an affirmative vote, and if it didn't, regardless of how interesting it might be, it would be rejected. Budgets would be easier to plan because money would be set aside in the budget to fund the activities that would fulfill the vision. The structure of the church would also be simplified. Only those organizations that are necessary for the completion of the vision would exist, and other committees and boards could be eliminated, freeing up people's time so they could focus on the truly important activities in the church.

There are many benefits from discerning God's vision for one's church, but there is one downside. Once the pastor understands God's vision for his or her church, he or she then becomes responsible for that vision. There are no longer any acceptable excuses. The pastor must now lead the church in the fulfillment of that vision, and he or she will be held accountable by God and the church to do so. Believe me, it's a lot easier and less risky to plead ignorance, at least in the short term.

Leadership Involves Risk

It is highly unlikely that God will give a church a vision to maintain the status quo. Vision will almost always involve change, and change will always include risk. Leadership in a twenty-first-century church requires willingness to take risks. Every decision a leader makes will require the leader to weigh the risks of change with the risks of taking no action. The leader must determine which presents the greater risk to the church before deciding which direction to go.

Such assessment does not guarantee success. In fact, leaders often fail. John Maxwell tells us that entrepreneurs average failing 3.8 times before becoming successful in business.[15] Leadership expert Max DePree claims that leaders are only right half of the time.[16] This means they are wrong the other half. For a visionary leader, that is all right. It's not that they want to be wrong or to fail, but they understand that there will be setbacks on their journey to success. Viewed correctly, each failure is a stepping-stone to eventual success, but many pastors do not view failure that way.

Churches and pastors are often very risk-averse. They see failure as . . . well, failure. In some churches it doesn't take too many failures before the congregation begins thinking about new leadership. It becomes easier for the pastor to play it safe. If one doesn't try new things, there is less risk of failure. Of course, there is also less chance of success, but many pastors don't plan on staying around to see any long-term success anyway.

One thing is clear from Scripture—the disciples of Christ refused to play it safe, especially after Jesus' resurrection. They went publicly into the marketplaces and synagogues preaching the name of Jesus despite being threatened, beaten, and eventually martyred. They didn't get it right every time. Paul and Barnabas got into a major disagreement over John Mark (see Acts 15:36-41) that became so contentious, they separated. The early church was convinced that Gentile converts to Christianity had to follow the laws and customs of Judaism until Paul, Barnabas, and Peter convinced them that God had saved the Gentiles apart from the Law (see vv. 1-29). Peter was rebuked by both Jesus Christ (see Matt. 16:21-23) and Paul (see Gal. 2:11-14) for impulsive behavior. I doubt these are the only times they failed, but they didn't let setbacks stop them. They learned from their mistakes and moved forward until they had turned the world upside down.

We need pastors who are willing to take risks to advance the kingdom of God, and we need churches who are willing to allow such risks. Playing it safe in the twenty-first century won't get the job done. One of the questions we have to ask is whether or not we love people enough to take the risks necessary to reach them for Christ. Leonard Ravenhill, who never pulled his punches, wrote, "This generation of preachers is responsible for this generation of sinners. At the very door of our churches are the masses—unwon because they are unreached, unreached because they are unloved."[17]

We Need Pastors Who Are Willing to Lead

Churches are not going to change unless they have pastors who are committed to providing them with strong, spiritual, servant leadership. All three of these qualities are essential for a pastor to be a productive leader. First, it must be strong leadership. That does not mean dictatorial leadership. A strong leader is one who knows where he or she is going, has developed a strategy to get there, and is committed to taking as many on the trip as possible. As John Maxwell says, "Leaders need to remember that the point of leading is not to cross the finish line first. It's to take people across the finish line with you."[18] Dictators tend to lose a lot of people along the way.

One of the things that make a strong leader so effective is that other leaders will follow him or her. Leaders will not follow someone who is weaker than they are. Pastors can attract other leaders and followers, but most pastors only seem to attract followers. If we attract other leaders, we can accomplish more in our churches. In fact, the heart cry of many churches is for more leaders. If these churches cannot attract leaders and they are not doing anything intentional to develop leaders, where do they expect to find the leadership they need? We really need to do both—attract and develop leaders—but neither will happen if the pastor is not already a strong leader. A church very quickly begins to mirror its pastor, and if the pastor isn't willing to lead, or can't, it is highly unlikely that anyone else in the church, except the controllers, will assume a leadership role.

In addition to being strong, pastors must be spiritual leaders. "To be a spiritual leader means to be a person of spiritual maturity first, a leader second. And the only path to spiritual maturity is time spent in prayer, study, reflection, solitude, and service."[19] Timothy Geoffrion writes, "Only one base is adequate for Christian leadership—a vital spiritual life in which God is transforming us as individuals, and is leading and working through us as leaders."[20]

Let's be very honest here. Most pastors can do an adequate job in ministry by relying only on their own knowledge and abilities. In many churches, an adequate job is enough. However, no pastor should be content with doing an adequate job. There will come a time when our work will be judged by Someone with much higher standards than those found in many churches. Will our work be found to consist of hay, straw, and stubble, or gold, silver, and precious stones? The first three will be consumed in the final judgment while only the last three will be purified.

Pastors can only achieve their full potential in ministry when they allow God to transform their lives, and such transformation only occurs when we spend sufficient time with him and yield ourselves to his control. It is when we grow deeper in our relationship with God that we become more effective in our ministries. As others see their pastor growing deeper with God and the transformation that takes place as a result, many will also want to grow in their own walk with God.

It is only when a pastor becomes a spiritual leader that he or she is able to also become a servant leader. Servant leaders have three distinct qualities. First, they truly love the people God has given them. Second, they know and accept who they are. Finally, they understand that they ultimately serve God, not people.[21] I am convinced that unspiritual leaders are unlikely to have any of these qualities. How often have you heard a pastor complain about the people in his or her church, sometimes in very derogatory terms?

Most unspiritual pastors are not very accepting of who they are or where they are. One such pastor complained to me about how unfair it was that he completed seminary and had to serve in a bivocational church. Such pastors also do not know who they serve or they wouldn't be changing churches every two or three years. After years of hearing pastors tell how God has led them to one church then another, I sometimes wonder how confused God must be. To hear them talk, it sounds like even God can't figure out where they are supposed to serve!

Being a servant leader does not come naturally to most people. We have been conditioned to look out for our own interests, not those of other people. Too many pastors climb the ministerial ladder to achieve the success they believe they deserve. However, it does us no good to climb the ladder of success if when we get to the top we find it is leaning against the wrong building. What is God's vision for your life and ministry? How does God define success for you? It may be in a megachurch in a large city or it could be in a small, rural church between two mountains. A genuine servant leader will serve where God places him or her, will love the people in that place, and will be grateful to be called by God to that place of ministry.

The Challenge to Pastors and Congregations

Pastors, do you have a heart for strong, spiritual, servant leadership? This is a critical question. If not, I believe you should not be a pastor. You can fill other ministry roles, but you should not be a pastor because pastors must lead the church if it is to effectively impact its community for the kingdom of God. Strong, effective congregations only exist when there is a pastor who is a strong leader. Without a strong leader, good leaders will leave the church and dysfunctional people will take over,[22] and this never leads to a healthy, effective congregation. If you are the pastor, you must lead.

Congregations, the other side of the coin is that you must allow pastors to lead. Do not expect your pastor to lead the church while you are standing on the brake. Not every decision has to be put to a vote. I say that as a lifelong Baptist, and Baptists vote on everything! And then we wonder why things seldom change in our churches and why so many of our churches are in decline. A former professor of church history at a Baptist seminary wrote, "One will scan the pages of the New Testament in vain for wide evidence of majority control of church matters. There is no account of a congregation deciding by majority vote what the will of God was or what 'truth' was. There are, on the other hand, numerous references to the apostles' meeting to decide doctrine, apostles giving orders, and apostles overseeing congregations and the Church at large."[23]

I am convinced that in the twenty-first-century church we must either decide we are going to trust our leaders and God to make the decisions that will lead our churches forward, or we will miss important ministry opportunities while we wait for committees to hold one meeting after another trying to decide what to do. The world is moving too fast for the church to continue doing business as usual. If we cannot trust our leadership to make the right decisions, we probably do not have the right people in those positions, and if we cannot trust God to guide our leaders, then we have even greater problems.

A congregation's lack of trust in its leaders and the pastor's lack of leadership further demonstrate the disease that exists in the body of Christ. It is keeping our churches from having significant impact on today's world. This must change if the church is to once again become the church that God envisioned.

Summary

The issue of pastoral leadership is challenging for many pastors and churches. Many pastors have never been trained to lead, have little interest in leading, and see their role as managers and enablers. Many churches, especially those with a congregational polity, do not expect the pastor to lead. Although they may say he or she is the leader of their church, in reality the pastor is a manager, not a leader. In such churches, even if the pastor attempted to lead, he or she would not be allowed to do so. These churches are run by committees and boards, and final decisions are made by congregational vote. To allow the pastor and a core of other leaders to make the majority of decisions without congregational approval would be a huge paradigm shift for these churches. I challenge churches to make just such a shift.

The existing structure of committees and congregational vote worked well in a more settled church, but in the twenty-first century things are moving so rapidly that the church must become more fluid in its decision making. Decisions need to be made rapidly or opportunities will be missed. Our churches need pastors who can lead their churches to respond quickly to ministry opportunities, and our churches need to be willing to follow their pastor's leadership to meet those needs.

This takes us back to one of my earlier questions: Who are we here for? If our churches simply exist for the benefit of their members, then all we need are managers to maintain what we have and to meet the needs of our existing members. If we answer that we are also here for those who have not yet been reached with the Gospel of Jesus Christ, then we need to become willing to follow the leadership of those appointed to those positions. We must take the risk of following that leadership if we are to effectively reach those we are currently not reaching. The answer to that question will say much about the condition of the church's heart.

5

A Lack of Discipled Believers

Turning church members into disciple-makers—
disciples who make other disciples—is one of the
most pressing challenges of our time.[1]
—Bill Easum

DISCIPLESHIP is a word that is often used but seldom understood. What do we really mean when we say we want to make disciples, and how is a disciple made? Are there three easy steps to discipleship? six? ten? What does a disciple look like? How does one know if one has become a disciple? These are questions that few churches have taken time to answer.

Definition of a Disciple

Fortunately, Randy Pope has asked these questions about discipleship. Pope is the senior pastor of Perimeter Church in Duluth, Georgia. Despite the growth of his church, Pope realized they, like many churches, had focused on the process of discipleship without ever defining what a disciple should look like. He challenged the church leadership to create an image of a disciple, which they did. Their conclusion is as follows.

A mature and equipped follower of Christ is one who:

- lives consistently under the control of the Holy Spirit, the direction of the Word of God, and the compelling love of Christ;
- has discovered, developed, and is using his or her spiritual gifts;
- has learned to effectively share his or her faith while demonstrating radical love that amazes the world it touches; and
- gives strong evidence of being:
  - a faithful member of Christ's church
  - an effective manager of life, relationships, and resources
  - a willing minister to God's people and
  - an available messenger to nonkingdom people

In addition, the mature, equipped follower of Christ demonstrates a life characterized as

- gospel driven

- morally pure
- discipleship grounded
- socially responsible
- worship focused
- evangelistically bold
- family faithful[2]

At first glance it seems that this is a lot to ask of a person, but being a disciple of Jesus Christ does demand a lot. To go from being an unbeliever to a fully functioning disciple of Christ requires a complete transformation. That is why many churches never really get serious about discipleship. They know many of the people in their congregations are not interested in such a complete transformation. Too many Christians are like the one quoted by Wilber Rees.

I would like to buy $3 worth of God, please, not enough to explode my soul or disturb my sleep, but just enough to equal a cup of warm milk or a snooze in the sunshine. I don't want enough of Him to make me love a black man or pick beets with a migrant. I want ecstasy, not transformation; I want the warmth of the womb, not a new birth. I want a pound of the Eternal in a paper sack. I would like to buy $3 worth of God, please.[3]

The Problem

I recently spoke with a pastor who announced he was moving to another church to serve. Because I would be working with the pastor search committee for this church, I asked him what he believed to be the church's primary need. He immediately replied that more of the congregation needed to become serious about being disciples of Jesus Christ. The majority in that church were content to attend worship services on Sunday, if nothing interfered, and feel they had done all that should be expected of them. Sunday school attendance was declining in that church, and despite the departing pastor's best efforts, there was very little interest in any small-group meetings that could help one grow spiritually. In addition, there were a number of people in the congregation who could only be called "mean-spirited." Since I met some of them in the past, I had to agree with him. If they were asked, they would say they are growing as disciples of Jesus Christ, but there is little or no fruit evident in their lives. Unfortunately, this is all too common in many of our churches.

At a gathering of judicatory leaders, there was a discussion about one of the fast-growing churches in their state. An individual representing that judicatory spoke up and said that the church is growing rapidly in its worship attendance, but he also noted that attendance in their Christian education program was declining at about the same pace the worship attendance was growing. He said this is common among many churches and believed it would lead to serious problems within the next ten to twenty years. As he explained, the new members who are doing little to grow spiritually will become the next generation of leaders in their churches. He fears they will attempt to lead their churches from a business perspective because that will be all they know.

This is not a new problem for the church. Puritan pastor Richard Baxter challenged the believers in his day about this same issue. "Were you but as willing to get the knowledge of God and heavenly things as you are to know how to work your trade, you would have set yourself to it before this day, and you would have spared no cost or pains till you had got it. But you account seven years little enough to learn your trade, and will not bestow one day in seven in diligent learning the matters of your salvation."[4]

For the future well-being of the church, it is imperative that the church begin to take seriously the call to make disciples. The Great Commission does not simply say to lead people to make a decision for Jesus Christ or to baptize people. In the Great Commission, Christ commands us to "make disciples of all the nations" (Matt. 28:19). The challenge is to take a person who does not know God and has little interest in him and help that individual become a fully devoted follower. It is nothing less than a complete life transformation, and the question must be, how will the church successfully help people make such a transformation?

What Isn't Working?

When many churches think of discipleship, they first think of their Sunday school programs. At this point I like to ask my Dr. Phil question: How is that working for you? Most of the time when he asks that question on his television program he already knows what the person is doing is not working, and he asks that question to help the individual realize the same thing. So, church leader, how is what you are currently doing working for you? Is your Sunday school program producing the transformation in your church members that would be expected of a disciple of Jesus Christ? For many churches the answer is no.

The fact that we even expect our Sunday school to produce disciples indicates a mistaken concept of discipleship. We often equate being a disciple with acquiring knowledge. Learning more about God and the teachings of Scripture is important but does not automatically lead to one becoming a disciple. Milfred Minatrea understands this when he writes, "Religious systems have long specialized in the transfer of spiritual knowledge, but they have an equally long heritage of producing enlightened followers whose lifestyles remain unchanged by that spiritual knowledge."[5] God didn't give us the Bible just so we could gain knowledge; he gave it so his people could be transformed.[6] This transformation is not occurring in many Christians' lives.

If only one of three church people are passing the school of Christian maturity, their churches are failing for two principle reasons: First, we've assumed that by concentrating on educating children, Christian adults would result. Someone said that

Jesus played with children and taught adults, while churches try to teach children and play with adults. Second, we assumed that the way you educate children (or those older) is by teaching about the Bible, about Jesus, about church history, about Christian morality, and so forth. With these assumptions, churches believed that all they needed were trained teachers, objective subject matter, attractive curriculum, up-to-date supplies and equipment, and age-graded classes in separate classrooms to get the desired result. At best, we now have church members struggling to be Christian and, at worst, poorly educated atheists.[7]

I am not opposed to age-graded Sunday school classes, but it is important to remember that Sunday school is less than 250 years old. This means that the church successfully discipled its members by other means for much of its history. We should not become locked into one program and believe it is the only way to accomplish things. Sunday school has been a useful tool since its inception, and it continues to have value for some people today, but for the postmodern believer it won't be enough to help him or her become a fully devoted follower of Jesus Christ.

Discipleship Is Caught, Not Taught

Learning about the Bible is great, and we have too many believers who are biblically illiterate. That should not be. However, education alone is not enough to make one a disciple. Practicing spiritual disciplines such as prayer, fasting, meditation, and more are necessary, but none of them are enough to qualify us as disciples of Christ. To truly be disciples of Jesus, the church must connect daily life with other spiritual resources.[8] We must live out what we have learned in the ordinary moments of life. It is in the ups and downs of life that one grows into discipleship and experiences true transformation. The church's challenge is to teach people how to apply what they have learned particularly through ministry opportunities.

Here is where the missional church has a huge advantage over the maintenance-minded church. Maintenance-minded churches affirm the traditional teachings of the faith, ask people to serve on committees and boards, see mission as something done by other people in some distant place, and focus on their own needs. Everything is placed neatly in its own little compartment.

The missional church is different in that people are challenged to flesh out their beliefs in action. Every member is expected to be involved in ministry. One of my favorite definitions of a missional church is that it is "a reproducing community of authentic disciples, being equipped as missionaries sent by God, to live and proclaim His Kingdom in their world."[9] Learning is not seen as an end in itself but something that is to be lived out in society as a way of impacting one's culture for God. Discipleship occurs both through learning and through opportunities to use that learning in service.

This may be one reason why so many churches struggle to develop genuine disciples: they do not provide them with sufficient opportunities to be involved in ministry. In a typical maintenance-minded church, the pastor, staff, or both are expected to minister to the congregation. Members see themselves as consumers and evaluate the pastor on how well he or she delivered the goods. This is the mind-set of people who leave a church because "they no longer feel fed in this church." These individuals have no idea that they have been called do more than sit in a pew waiting for a minister to feed them. They may attend every Bible study offered by the church, but until they become involved in doing something with what they have learned they will continue to be stunted in their spiritual growth.

Jesus' invitation to those who would become his disciples was "Follow me." He then took them on a journey that shaped them for the rest of their lives and prepared them for the battles they would face. That journey included both times of teaching and times of hands-on ministry. Very quickly the disciples found themselves on the front lines of battle, and some of the battles became learning opportunities that continued to impact them as long as they lived.

Which is more likely to help develop a disciple: sitting in an air-conditioned Sunday school class studying the latest statistics on hunger in the United States or spending a Saturday working at a shelter preparing meals for homeless people? Which will help a person grow deeper in his or her spiritual walk: talking about the importance of missionary work overseas or spending a week working on a youth center in Cap Haïtien, Haiti? I can tell you the week I spent in Haiti impacted me far more than a year's worth of Sunday school classes ever did.

This does not mean we do not need the educational component in our disciple-making. The classroom experience is important. Every believer needs the education to be well-grounded in his or her faith. I am stressing that church education programs are not enough to develop disciples. Hands-on ministry experiences must complement the classroom experience. Jesus is our example here. He not only taught the Twelve but also sent them out to do ministry. His teaching and the ministry experience combined were meant to develop them as disciples. It is vital that we provide ministry opportunities for people in our churches if we want them to grow as disciples.

Discipleship Is Messy

One of the reasons many churches struggle with discipling their members is that discipleship is messy. It's easier to place people in age-graded classrooms and have a promotion Sunday each year to move people to the next age class. It's appealing to order slick, multicolored literature for each class with a teacher's guide to make it easier to prepare a lesson each week. It's often easier for the pastor to tend to ministry needs himself or herself instead of calling a congregation member to minister to that need. It's messy to have a variety of people involved in ministry throughout the community.

This leads to some important questions: how do you know when people are ready to serve? Can they be trusted to do it right? What happens if they say the wrong thing? Will it impact the community's perception of the church if they really mess up?

The fact is, nobody knows if your congregation is ready to minister until the opportunity arises, and there are no guarantees anyone will do it right. Notice Jesus didn't worry about that with his disciples. In fact, if we believe that he is omniscient, we would have to believe he knew they would struggle at times to get it right, but he sent them out to minister anyway.

For instance, the disciples attempted to cast a demon out of a young boy and were unable to do so. After Jesus cast out the demon, the disciples came to him privately and asked why they had not been able to do the same. Very bluntly, Jesus told them their failure was due to unbelief (see Matt. 17:14-21). Another time, Jesus challenged them to feed the multitude who had been listening to his teaching. Their immediate response was that they had no food for so many people. Jesus took what food they had, blessed it, and had the disciples pass it to the people. Everyone ate until full, and there were twelve baskets of food remaining, one for each of the disciples to hold while they wondered about what they had just witnessed (see Luke 9:12-17). The disciples' biggest failure occurred on the night Jesus was arrested when they all ran away from the soldiers, leaving Jesus there alone (see Mark 14:50).

The disciples got it wrong many times, and I am sure their mistakes caused some people in Israel to get the wrong idea about Christ and those who followed him. But they learned from their mistakes. They learned to trust more in God and the leadership of his Spirit. Christ used their mistakes to teach them about the kingdom of God. The disciples went from making a lot of mistakes to being known as people who turned the world upside down, and the world is still being impacted by the work they did nearly two thousand years ago. Yes, discipleship is messy, but it is in the messiness that we grow and develop, and we learn that God can minister even in the midst of the mess.

Pastors Must Let Go

Too many pastors still see their role as the provider of all ministry to the church. This lone-ranger mentality will not work in the twenty-first century. There is simply too much ministry that needs to occur for any one person to do it alone. Pastors must develop ministry teams within the church and equip them to do the work. Ministry must be seen as something to be done together. Over thirty-five years ago, Robert Munger wrote:

> In our time it may well be that the greatest single bottleneck to the renewal and outreach of the church is the division of roles between clergy and laity that results in a hesitancy of the clergy to trust the laity with significant responsibility, and in turn a reluctance on the part of the laity to trust themselves as authentic ministers of Christ, either in the church or outside the church.[10]

This is no less true today.

Greg Ogden observes that the first Reformation gave the Bible to the people, and the second reformation will give the ministry to the people.[11] This reformation is happening in churches across North America, and it is one that must include all churches if we are to effectively take the kingdom of God into our communities. For many traditional churches, this is a paradigm shift that will not be easy to make, and it will require some major changes in their expectations and how they function. One necessary change is for pastors to intentionally equip their congregations to do ministry. This will be the twenty-first-century model of discipleship. Discipleship will no longer be seen as the accumulation of knowledge and information about God and the Bible, nor will it be enough for one to be involved in church committees and boards. A disciple of Jesus Christ will be one who has been equipped to use his or her God-given gifts to serve and fulfill his or her purpose in life.

The primary equippers in each church are the pastors and teachers (see Eph. 4:11-12). At this point language becomes important. What do we call the pastor who is committed to lead a church focused on discipleship and lay ministry development? If the pastor is called *the* minister, it is implied that others in the church are not ministers. This is the problem we have in many of our modern churches today. I've always liked the term "preacher" because I see that as a fundamental responsibility of the pastor, but that really does not do justice to all that a discipling pastor does. Even the word "pastor" has baggage for some people, but it is still a good term to describe the overall ministry a pastor does. But I wonder if another term might be even more appropriate as the church marches further into the twenty-first century.

The word I'm thinking of is "coach," and to be more precise an even better term might be "player-coach." I don't want people to think of a pastor-coach as one who stands on the sidelines shouting out instructions to the players. A player-coach is one who is involved in the game along with his or her fellow teammates, and this should describe the role of the pastor.

Now, I am not suggesting that pastors go out and change their business cards or the church sign out front. I think many people would struggle with calling their pastor "coach," but I am suggesting that this might be a preferable way for pastors to see their work. "Coaching . . . enables transformation, which in turn leads to missional ministry."[12] Christian psychologist Gary Collins writes, "Coaching helps people expand their vision, build their confidence, unlock their potential, increase their skills, and take practical steps towards their goals."[13] Isn't this another way of talking about discipleship? I should hasten to say that both sources quoted here are talking about coaching in a Christian context, and such coaching is more apt to help a person become a fully functioning disciple of Jesus Christ than merely asking them to sit in a class or a small group for an hour each week.

This is a paradigm shift that many pastors will resist, in large part because it is so foreign to them. We've been trained to lead worship and provide pastoral care and promote programs. Most of us have not been trained to coach others and to invite them to do ministry with us. A couple of years ago I was talking with some ministry colleagues and said that I felt I had a very good pastoral ministry at my former church. However, if I ever felt led to leave the judicatory ministry I was now doing, I could not go back and do pastoral ministry as I had for twenty years. I admitted to them that my fear was that I would not know how to do ministry in a way that would be meaningful in the twenty-first century. I think many who have been in ministry for some time share that fear.

Many pastors will also find this shift frightening because it challenges their sense of identity. Our pastoral identities are often found in those things that separate us from our congregations. We are seen as the theological experts, the ones who are onstage each Sunday during the worship hour, and the ones who are called upon to pray when a family member is dying or when the potato salad needs blessing at the annual potluck dinner. We are the go-to people in our congregations, and this will be very hard for some to give up because of their great need to be needed.

Part of our problem is that we have failed to realize that equipping others to do ministry is one of the primary purposes of the pastor. Go back and reread Ephesians 4:11-12. Reread the Great Commission too. We are not just to reach the world for Jesus Christ; we are to help those who are reached become fully functioning disciples of Jesus Christ. In recent decades we have lost sight of this and made equipping a specialty in ministry. This is not supposed to be the work of a few specialists who have been trained specifically to do this work; it is the work of everyone called to pastoral ministry. Pastor, your primary task is to equip God's people to do the ministry he has gifted them to do. Greg Ogden says it so clearly when he writes, "The rediscovered role of pastors in our day is not to do ministry for those who are passive recipients of their care, but to empower the body through the avenues of the pastors' individual gifts and to call forth every person's potential for ministry."[14]

People Must Want to Become Disciples

The lack of discipleship in many churches is not entirely the fault of pastors. There are many Christians sitting in churches Sunday after Sunday who have no interest in becoming fully functioning disciples of Jesus Christ. They want to be consumers enjoying the benefits of church membership, but they do not want to accept the responsibilities of membership. They may be willing to serve on a committee or help out occasionally in a special program, but they are not interested in committing to a life of discipleship. To understand this, let's briefly look at the differences between being a church member and being a disciple.

Church membership is all about rights and privileges. If you are a member of a country club, you might get to play golf or tennis there for free. You can attend club dinners and other activities, and you can vote on club issues. Being a member of a church is similar. In many churches you receive free weddings for your children and a free funeral when your time comes. As a member you get to select the music used during the worship services, the times services will be held, and you get to vote on the budget and other issues that come before the congregation. You are a member, and you have rights.

Being a disciple isn't about enjoying one's rights. In fact, for a disciple it is more about responsibilities than rights. A disciple understands he or she has a responsibility to be a good steward of all God has provided. Financially, that means a disciple tithes his or her income to the church—and that is enough right there to keep many people from taking the call to discipleship seriously. Being a disciple also includes being faithful stewards of our God-given gifts and talents. Rather than being content to sit on a committee or board, a disciple seeks to be involved in a worthwhile ministry that makes a difference in the lives of others. They are willing to spend the time necessary to have their gifts fine-tuned so they can be more effective in ministry.

Disciples are also committed to their churches. "There is no such thing as a solitary disciple . . . Important discipleship experiences may occur outside the bounds of congregational life, but disciples always come from and return to the community."[15] Disciples do not attend church services when convenient; they schedule their lives around them. They seek out opportunities to learn more about God, the Bible, and their own personal call from God, and many of these opportunities will come through their local church. A person once told me that she never felt closer to God than when she took a walk in the outdoors. She was explaining why she was so irregular in her church attendance. I do not doubt her ability to worship God alone in the outdoors, but I do doubt her ability to grow as a disciple. The Bible teaches that we are not to forsake the assembling of ourselves with other believers (see Heb. 10:25). There are many good reasons for that admonition, and one of them is so that we can grow and mature as disciples of Jesus Christ.

A discipled life is one that is centered on Christ, not on oneself, and that is another reason why so many are not interested in becoming disciples. "There is a price to be paid for becoming Christ-centered. The fully surrendered life requires the denial of self. This is a high price for us since, from birth, we are self-centered people."[16] Perhaps we need to be reminded of the even higher price that God paid to redeem us to himself. When we refuse to become disciples, we put our own pleasures and comforts above the call God has given each of us. This reveals a lack of gratitude for being in his family. In short, it shows a serious problem of the heart.

The refusal of so many of God's people to become fully functioning disciples of Jesus Christ is behind many of the problems in our churches today and is the reason we have such little impact on society. In nearly thirty years of ministry I have seen many church fights and more than a few splits. Not once have I seen any of these fights led by growing disciples of Christ. I have seen pastors treated worse than slaves and several terminated by immature, childish church members who refused to grow up and become mature followers of Christ. I see church after church led by carnal leaders who can't understand why no one is attracted to their church. They fire one pastor after another, certain that they will eventually find one who can grow their church, never realizing that their own spiritual immaturity is the primary reason why people from the community avoid their church. Such people should stop long enough to notice that not even their own children attend their church once they get old enough to make that decision. These children have seen through the hypocrisy of their parents and want nothing to do with their church, and in too many instances, even their Christian beliefs.

At workshops, pastors often ask me what they should do with those in their churches who do not want to grow and become disciples. Sometimes they are the people who make up the bulk of the leadership in the church. My response is always the same: you have to ride the horses that want to run. You cannot force a Christian to want to become a disciple. If God can't get them to make that choice, neither can a pastor. And a pastor often can't control who is currently in leadership positions in the church. Especially in smaller churches, the same people may have been in the same leadership positions for decades, and a new pastor is not going to change that. They may be the most immature, irresponsible, weak Christians you have ever seen, but there is little you will be able to do about it. If you try to force them out of their positions, there is only one person who will be leaving, and it will be you.

A better solution is to identify people in your church who want to grow and will make good future leaders, then invest in their spiritual development. I am not suggesting you ignore the immature Christians who do not want to grow. Continue to pastor them, love them, minister to them, just be sure to invest yourself in those who want to go deeper with God. Prepare them so they will be ready when leadership positions begin to open up.

If you do this, however, expect attacks from the immature members of your congregation. You will be accused of having a clique and of ignoring others. You will be accused of playing favorites with a few and abandoning the majority.

When those attacks come, just remember you are following a pretty good example. Jesus had many disciples, but he invested most of his time and teaching into a core of twelve. He spoke in parables to the masses, but he explained the parables to the Twelve (see Luke 8:10). These were the ones to whom he gave the greatest responsibility—taking the message of his resurrection to the world.

There were times, however, when Jesus narrowed the Twelve down to only three who seemed to make up his inner circle: Peter, James, and John. He took only them when he went up on the Mount of Transfiguration, when he raised the girl from the dead, and when he went into the Garden of Gethsemane to pray just before he was arrested. "Jesus' model teaches pastors that one essential way to carry out ministry is to invest in a few who in turn can be equipped to invest in others. It requires vision to think small and to anticipate the long-term impact."[17] It not only takes vision but takes courage as well. An equipping pastor must accept being misunderstood by some. To find that courage, a pastor must ask which is more important: gaining the approval of the masses, or equipping disciples who will continue to make an impact long after the pastor is gone.

Discipleship Must Be Intentional

It is not the purpose of this volume to provide a discipleship plan. There are many other resources available to assist church leaders with such a plan. However, I must emphasize that discipleship is not going to just happen automatically. A pastor and church must be very intentional about discipleship. Many churches may need two plans: one for established Christians and another for new believers. If I could only start with one, I would start with the new members. It is imperative that a church have an intentional plan in place to properly assimilate people into the Christian life. Give them high expectations right from the beginning of their Christian experience, and have a plan to help them achieve those expectations.

I believe three ingredients are necessary for every church's plan. One, people need to be taught. We cannot expect people to grow as disciples if they do not know Scripture or how to put their faith into practice. Two, they need to have an opportunity to develop relationships with people in the congregation. Except in the smallest churches, this often best occurs in small groups. There are many ways to do small groups, and a church that is intentional about discipleship should regularly create new small groups for people to join. Very seldom are people interested in joining an existing group. They are much more likely to join a new group. The third ingredient is to provide everyone with an opportunity for hands-on ministry. Such involvement is essential for one to grow as a disciple. Every person who expresses an interest in joining a church should be told up-front that these three things are expected of every member.

As you formulate a discipleship plan, do not limit yourself to thinking in terms of how you were discipled. One of the problems in many churches is they want to relive what worked in the past, not realizing that just because something worked well at one time does not mean that it will work well now. David Ray challenges us to begin by thinking about the end product. He says we should ask, "What kind of people and churches are we trying to develop?"[18] Once we have a clear goal, we can put together a plan that will transform the people in our church.

Summary

Discipleship is not an option for people who are committed to living for Jesus Christ. It is expected of every person who invites Christ into his or her life. Individuals have a responsibility to grow as disciples, and churches have the responsibility to provide growth opportunities. Such opportunities will include both instruction and practicing what has been learned. To become a discipling church, a paradigm shift will have to occur. Pastors must learn to let go of traditional ways of viewing pastoral ministry and begin to focus on their biblical responsibility to equip believers to do ministry themselves. At the same time, members of the congregation must take responsibility for ministering to one another and those outside the church, and they must be willing to be trained in how to minister.

A church that takes discipleship seriously will benefit in many ways. Believers will grow as they learn more about their God-given gifts and how to use them, and the surrounding community will benefit as it is impacted by believers living out their faith. The church will grow as people are brought into the kingdom of God through the shared efforts of the congregation.

6

A Lack of Denominational Excellence

At the core of my conclusions is a belief that
mainline denominations will survive only if their
leaders realize that the time is past for them to
function as programming bureaucracies.[1]

—Tony Campolo

DENOMINATIONS are facing tough times. Many are struggling financially because their churches financially support outside ministries rather than denominational ones. Denominations and judicatories have been forced to restructure their staff due to budget restraints. Many of the resources that used to come from denominational headquarters are now being provided by the middle judicatories or have been eliminated completely.

Missionaries have not escaped the financial challenges facing the denominations. In the past, American Baptist missionaries did not have to raise financial support. Sufficient funds came into the denomination through its various offerings to support the work of their missionaries. That is no longer the case. Today, missionaries are required to raise a substantial portion of their own support. In essence, we have made our denomination's missionaries independent.

Reduced Importance Given to Denominations

For a long time commitment to denominations has been in decline. This is true of both individuals and churches. There was a time when a family would move to a new community and would look for a church of the same denomination in which they were raised. That is less likely to happen today. People are looking for churches that meet their needs, regardless of the denominational label. As I mentioned before, my son and daughter both attended the church I pastored for many years, but neither of them attend a church in that denomination today. When they and their families were seeking a church, they looked for certain ministries, and the name of the denomination meant little. They are representative of many today.

Some churches with historic ties to denominations have backed away from those commitments in recent years. Some have completely severed their relationship due to conflict with denominational leadership, while others have made their relationship with the denomination less visible. In some cases, churches have changed their names to remove denominational labels that may discourage people from attending.

A number of churches have reduced support to their denomination because the benefits of being part of the denomination are decreasing. This may be more common among smaller churches who do not see their denominational leaders as often as they used to and often feel they have been abandoned to struggle along by themselves. I frequently hear comments such as this from bivocational ministers who feel unsupported by their denominational leadership.

Yet another reason denominations receive less support today than in the past is a shift in how people think about ministry. There was a time when ministry consisted of local churches performing the ministries (programs) mandated by the denomination. The pastors were educated and trained in denominational schools, towed the denominational line, and led their churches according to the denominational calendar. Money was regularly collected to send to the denomination for program development and missionary work around the world. Judicatories often distributed the programs from the denomination to the local churches and received money from the local churches to send back to the denomination. This has all changed in recent years.

There is a growing focus today on local church ministry. They do not believe they need a denomination to tell them how to minister because they know their own community far better than someone sitting in an office halfway across the country. The local church is taking the lead in planning the ministries they need. Denominations and judicatories are seen as supporting organizations to provide the churches with the resources they have requested, and if they cannot provide such resources, the churches look to other denominations or parachurch organizations. This paradigm shift will require most denominations and judicatories to undergo major changes or find themselves increasingly irrelevant to their churches. Denominations will require much less bureaucracy, and this streamlining will be very painful and perhaps impossible for some.

Divisive Issues

In addition to the situations mentioned above, another major reason churches are abandoning their denominations is disagreement over hot issues that have divided Christians for years. In the past, the hot issues often revolved around the authority of the Scripture or membership in organizations that some churches opposed, such as the World Council of Churches. Today, the two issues most likely to divide churches are abortion and homosexuality. Neither of these issues are likely to be resolved anytime soon, if ever.

In a July 2009 survey, the Gallup Poll found that 48 percent of those surveyed reported they were pro-choice and 45 percent said they were pro-life.[2] America is almost evenly divided over this issue, and we should not be surprised to find the same division in our churches and denominations.

A number of denominations have been forced to address the homosexual issue in recent years, especially as it relates to their clergy. Some have consistently voted against allowing practicing homosexuals to serve as clergy, while others now approve of ordaining homosexuals. At least one has installed a practicing homosexual in a high position, prompting a lot of turmoil within that denomination.

The denomination I serve has been accused of supporting the homosexual lifestyle despite a clear denominational statement that such a lifestyle is contrary to biblical teaching. The accusation comes because we have a few churches that support homosexuality, and our polity allows these churches to remain in our denomination despite holding beliefs that are contrary to our statement. As a result of this one issue, a large number of churches have withdrawn from the denomination. In 2006, the board of the American Baptist Churches of the Pacific Southwest region voted unanimously to withdraw from the denomination. This decision alone removed three hundred churches from the denomination, though a number of them have since associated with other regions in order to maintain their membership with the American Baptist Churches, USA.

These divisive issues will not go away until denominations make a firm decision about who they are and what they believe. As noted above, the United States is evenly divided on the abortion issue, and there is a growing acceptance of homosexuality. As I write this chapter, President Obama is seeking to reverse the "don't ask, don't tell" policy that prevents openly homosexual soldiers from serving in the military. Due to the growing acceptance of homosexual lifestyles, there has been little outcry about changing this policy. These issues are not going to be resolved by society, which means that they will continue to divide churches and denominations until each one determines where it will stand on each issue.

That is a problem for the many denominational leaders who focus more on political issues than being spiritual leaders. Seeking to be all things to all people, they become less and less important to anyone. They are so desperate to be inclusive and politically correct that they are unwilling to take a biblical stand when it is unpopular.

This relates to chapter 1 where we discussed the importance of making the Bible, not culture, our ultimate authority for belief and practice. Without a firm biblical base upon which to stand, we will fall for anything. This is true for individuals, for churches, and for denominations. More and more we find denominations led by people who are unwilling to take a biblical stand for anything. They remind me of the mayor who was asked what he thought about a certain issue. He responded, "Well, some of my friends are for this issue and some are against it." The reporter then asked, "Well, what do you think?" The mayor said, "I'm for my friends." It sounds like a typical politician's answer, and it's the same kind of nonanswer we often hear from denominational leaders unwilling to take a stand on controversial issues.

Ultimately, the battles over abortion and homosexuality are battles over biblical authority. Very clear biblical statements must be ignored to defend either abortion or the homosexual lifestyle. As important as the autonomy of the local church is, it comes in second place to biblical authority. Either one believes what the Bible says or one doesn't. If one believes what the Bible teaches about the sanctity of life and the homosexual lifestyle, then one will not be tempted to do all kinds of exegetical gymnastics to try to defend society's views on these issues. If one doesn't accept the authority of Scripture, then he or she isn't going to be concerned about what the Bible says about these issues anyway. Such a person has become his or her own authority on the issue.

Take a Stand

Here's a thought for denominational leaders: how about just deciding where you stand on an issue, then act on that decision? I'm tired of hearing denominational leaders claim they lack the authority to make changes on these issues. I understand that denominational authority is held by governing boards, but I also know that all leaders have the power of the pulpit at their disposal. They have a voice and a prophetical mandate to use that voice to call a denomination to biblical standards. They have many opportunities to voice their opinions on these issues, and they have a great impact on the decisions that boards make. We don't need more studies and more focus groups. We've studied these issues long enough. What we need are leaders with a spine who will call the denomination and its churches to a biblical standard.

Some readers will object to this on the grounds that this violates the autonomy of the local church and the priesthood of the believer. I too hold strongly to both of those concepts, but I also believe in the autonomy of the denomination. Let me explain. As an autonomous church, your congregation has the right to believe anything they want to. I would never try to take that freedom from you. But, as a denomination, an association of like-minded churches, we also have the right, and the responsibility, to determine what we believe and what your church must believe if it wants to be part of us. You can believe anything you want to, but you cannot believe anything you want to and be a member of a denomination that believes something completely opposite. Any denomination that permits that lacks integrity and is destined to ultimately fail.

There are many denominations that do not battle over these issues. They have very clear statements about abortion and homosexuality that their churches abide by. I find it very interesting that these denominations tend to be much stronger than the ones who won't take a stand on the issues, and these denominations also tend to be growing rather than declining. Of course, they have their own internal battles to address, but most of these battles are not due to a rejection of biblical authority.

If denominations ever hope to recover any measure of their former value to the kingdom of God, they are going to have to take a stand. I've often said that I just wish we would say where we stand on the issue of homosexuality, and in many ways I don't care which side of the issue we take. We should either say we support the right of every person to choose the lifestyle he or she wants, or we should say that the practice of homosexuality is wrong and if your church supports that lifestyle you can no longer be part of our denomination. Once the denomination takes a stand, then every church can decide for itself what to do as a result. We would lose churches regardless of which position we took, but we're losing churches anyway because we're not willing to take a stand. At least this way we would be losing churches because we took a position on an important issue.

My own denomination claims to have taken a position on this by pointing to our official statement that says the homosexual lifestyle is incompatible with the Christian lifestyle. Fine, but of what value is that statement if it isn't enforced? If we have churches who are ordaining homosexuals and affirming the homosexual lifestyle and nothing is being done about it, then the statement has no value at all.

Transforming a Denomination

Because my wife and I enjoy fishing, we bought a bass boat a few years ago. That boat was so much fun to drive, partially because it could turn on a dime. During the Vietnam War I spent three years on the USS *Enterprise,* at that time the largest warship in the world. It took miles to turn that huge ship around. Transforming a denomination will be much more like trying to turn an aircraft carrier around than turning around a bass boat. It will take years to make the changes that many denominations need to make.

A denomination is a bureaucracy, and we know that any bureaucracy will go to great lengths to maintain its current status. Even dying denominations are incredibly self-protective. They would rather die than change and will do everything possible to resist change. If it takes approximately five years to bring about a significant change in a congregation, it may take ten to twenty years to do the same in a denomination. As a result, few people are even interested in trying. Churches that oppose the denomination's position find it easier to leave than to stay and try to bring about the needed changes. Or as is more common, the churches simply ignore their denomination, focus on their own ministries, and let the denomination slowly fade away into oblivion.

Although changing a denomination seems almost impossible, there are people willing to do it, especially for the sake of the denomination's continuing vitality. However, those leading such an effort must understand that transformation will be costly, both to the denomination and to them as leaders. Lines will be drawn, struggles will occur, and relationships with some individuals within the denomination will be changed forever. It will be painful for everyone involved, but perhaps there will be less pain in such a transformation than there will be in seeing a denomination continue to shrink both in size and in spiritual power.

Rewards of Transformation

Rather than focusing on the pain of transformation, it might be more helpful to focus on the rewards that will come if a denomination is transformed from maintaining the status quo to becoming missional in its perspective and efforts. A church can be missional without the support of a denomination, and in fact, many churches have become missional even though they are part of a denomination that is entirely focused on its own survival. These churches may retain their historic denominational affiliation, but they are not waiting for their denominations to catch up to what they are doing. However, it is much easier for a church to become missional if it is supported by its denomination.

I recently spoke at a national gathering of a denomination that is committed to new church planting. There was an energy in that meeting that I often do not find in other denominational meetings. Numerous denominational resources were available that pertained to planting new churches and to evangelism. New churches were recognized in various meetings. Nationally known speakers not affiliated with this denomination led workshops that pertained to planting new churches, making guests feel welcome, and a host of other helpful topics, all designed to help the churches and denomination reach more people for Christ.

I noticed another thing in this meeting: there were a good percentage of younger people attending this denomination's annual meeting. At most denominational meetings I attend, the crowd is much older. I spoke to a number of these young people and found out they are pastors, many of them bivocational. They were excited about being a part of a denomination that was committed to starting new churches, being faithful in evangelism, and was focused on ministry rather than bogged down in controversy.

This denomination still has its share of problems and issues to work out, but it has not been sidetracked from fulfilling its mission of reaching people for Jesus Christ. I spoke with enough denominational leaders to know that they have their share of dissenters and disagreements, but this is not their focus. They address the issues when needed, and then return to the vision of the denomination. Also, there is no question where this denomination stands on the issues that have caused so much division in other denominations. They have taken a very clear stand on these issues and they are not going to compromise their position in order to appease a few churches that disagree. You can stand with them or you can find another organization to join, but they are not going to violate their principles or their theological understanding about these issues to keep churches from leaving. Their mission is to advance the kingdom of God, not to debate issues that were settled centuries ago in the clear teachings of Scripture.

This seems to be a much healthier way of doing denominational work than trying to appease every group that wants to belong. I mentioned above that I believe in the autonomy of the denomination just as I believe in the autonomy of the local church. Your church doesn't have to believe everything that the denomination believes, but the denomination is under no obligation to compromise its beliefs just to make your church happy. I have belonged to many organizations in my life and in every one of them I had to conform to their standards, beliefs, and practices. If I didn't want to, and sometimes I didn't, then I was free to leave, but if I wanted to remain a part of them it was up to me to change. The organization was not going to take time away from its purpose in order to appease me, and this should be the attitude of a healthy denomination.

A transformed denomination should invest its resources in fulfilling its mission rather than running around in circles trying to make everybody happy. Every denomination is feeling the financial pressure of the current down economy. Many have reduced their staff counts, sold property, and cut back on their programs in order to balance their budgets. Even that hasn't been enough for several denominations. They have fallen back on investments to raise enough cash to continue operating. Many predict that even if the economy does recover, many denominations will never achieve the level of financial prosperity they once knew. As a result of this recession, many believe that people will become more frugal in their spending and giving habits. Many people saw denominations as unimportant even before the economic downturn began, and this isn't likely to change when the economy recovers. In postmodern America, people are more interested in giving to specific individuals or ministries they trust rather than to some general "mission fund" overseen by unknown persons at the denominational headquarters. These reasons alone probably mean the denominational coffers will never receive the kind of support they once had. This makes it even more critical to use these resources wisely—toward the fulfillment of the denomination's vision for ministry, not on efforts to satisfy everyone.

A Clear Vision

Most denominations have a vision statement, but that doesn't mean they have a vision for ministry. It's easy to put the right words on a piece of paper; it's much more difficult to live out those words. It is just as important for a denomination to have a clear vision for ministry as it is for a church. Otherwise, both organizations will drift around in circles and accomplish little.

Every denomination has a vision of some kind. Even a denomination that is focused on maintenance has a vision. Its vision is survival—to put enough grease on the wheels of the organization to keep them turning. The bureaucracy maintains the status quo, and if need be, hires lawyers to squelch any attempts at transformation.

The problem is that such a denomination has no heart, at least for the things that matter most to God. Remember that the mission of every church should be to fulfill the Great Commission and the Great Commandment. Therefore, if a denomination is to faithfully support its churches, it must support them in these two areas. The vision of the denomination must flow out of that purpose and become the driving force behind everything the denomination does.

Being on the same mission, however, does not mean each denomination's vision will be the same. A denomination that wishes to assist its churches in fulfilling the Great Commission may take differing approaches based on each church's needs. One denomination may focus much of its resources on planting new churches since most studies show that new churches tend to grow faster and attract more new people than existing churches. Another denomination may spend more time working with its existing churches to help them become healthier in the belief that a healthy body will be a growing body. A third denomination may assist its churches to move from a maintenance mind-set to a missional one that focuses on the spiritual and physical needs of their communities. A fourth denomination might focus on leadership development, especially in the areas of evangelism and church growth. Perhaps yet another denomination would notice that many of its churches are small and find it difficult to obtain seminary-trained leadership. This denomination could develop plans and resources to identify and train bivocational leaders. Of course, chances are that most denominations would not focus on only one aspect of assisting their churches and ignore the others. Many denominations would find it helpful to incorporate all these possibilities and more.

The important thing here is that these denominations would no longer be drifting along, addressing the same issues year after year and growing more and more irrelevant to their churches and to the world at large. They would have a focus, a purpose that is based on a clear understanding of a vision that is both biblical and relevant to the twenty-first century.

Will the Transition Happen?

Denominations have a better chance at transformation if they can do two things. First, they must hold a high view of Scripture. Our society today is doing everything it can to pull people away from any religious or moral teaching that is deemed politically incorrect. We must not allow society to determine what we believe or teach. Jesus said the church is to be salt and light to the world (see Matt. 5:13-14). Light exposes the darkness, and the church must expose the darkness of our society and its moral values. Although independent churches can be lights within their communities, much more is possible when denominations provide power for those lights to shine. That power requires a high view of Scripture not only from the pulpit but in seminaries and educational materials as well.

The second thing that must occur for denominational transformation is that each one must discover a fresh vision for the twenty-first century. As stated earlier, the *mission* hasn't changed, but the *vision* must change for any organization to effectively fulfill its purpose in this postmodern age. Denominations must learn that ministry occurs at the local church level and the primary reason for the denominational structure is to provide the resources their churches request. Denominations must have a global ministry as well, such as sending missionaries around the world and responding to national and international crises.

Many denominations will have to restructure themselves to see any real transformation occur. Large boards will need to be reduced in size to respond quickly with needed changes and to save money in a time of dwindling resources. A leaner organizational structure will quicken the decision making process and drive more of those decisions back to the local church and judicatory level, which is where many of these decisions should be made anyway. Again, local church leaders understand their communities much better than bureaucrats sitting in an office building half a country away. Other staffing cutbacks will affect both support personnel and people in leadership positions.

Because more will be expected of judicatory leadership there will have to be changes in the way they function as well. Judicatories have cut staff to the bare bones and are now being challenged with how to maintain their current ministries despite such reductions. This problem will only be compounded as denominations provide fewer resources and the judicatories are forced to make up the difference. Staff utilization takes up much of the planning time of these judicatories. Many of the things judicatories have done in the past will have to be relinquished so human and financial resources can be utilized in more productive ways. Such transformation will be painful but necessary if change is to succeed.

The judicatories that have trouble with these changes are the ones that are, in this outside observer's opinion, extremely bloated and inefficient. One denominational judicatory requires an enormous amount of mission dollars to maintain, and their churches receive little in return for that expenditure. This system could be streamlined, making more money available to mission work and the starting of new churches with little additional funds. However, there will be much opposition to such changes because too many people are benefiting from the current structure.

Evangelical denominations will find it easier to make the necessary changes than most mainline denominations, but such transformation will not come easy for any of them. Again, it comes down to a matter of the heart. Do the denominational leaders have a heart for mission or a heart that prefers the status quo? Do their hearts beat so passionately for mission that they are willing to do the hard work of transformation, or will they take the easy road to retirement and leave the hard work for others? In many ways it goes back to the question I often ask church leaders: who are we here for? Will we answer that question only with our lips, or will we answer that question from the depths of our hearts?

Summary

Some say the age of denominations has ended. People today are more apt to seek a church that can meet their individual needs than one affiliated with a particular denomination. Some churches have even eliminated from their names any obvious denominational ties. Despite all this, I don't think the age of denominations has ended.

Denominations with a clear ministry vision, a high regard for Scripture, and an ongoing effort to develop missionaries for home and abroad will continue to have a vital role to play in the kingdom of God. The good news is that many denominations are doing all these things and are healthy and extremely effective.

Denominations doing none of these things can either begin to transform themselves or continue to decline. Being mostly large bureaucracies, these denominations find transformation difficult, and so many will avoid it. Eventually, however, these denominations will recognize too late that they will soon be only a footnote in church history.

7

A Hardened Heart

And when He had looked around at them with
anger, being grieved by the hardness of their hearts,
He said to the man, "Stretch out your hand."
And he stretched it out, and his hand
was restored as whole as the other.

—Mark 3:5

IN THE ABOVE STORY, Jesus entered a synagogue and noticed a man with a deformed hand. We do not know if this man had been placed there intentionally by the religious leaders to test Jesus, but we do read that they intently watched him to see if he would violate their laws by healing the man on the Sabbath. We also do not know if Jesus purposely chose to heal the man to show the religious leaders that their laws regarding the Sabbath honored neither God nor God's creation. What we do know is that Jesus asked the religious leaders whether it was lawful to do good on the Sabbath and he healed the man's crippled hand. We also know that afterward the religious leaders began to plot together how they might destroy him.

For the religious leaders of Jesus' day, religion was about keeping rituals and rules. In the Ten Commandments God had commanded the Israelites to honor the Sabbath and keep it holy. The Pharisees in the first century believed the best way to do that was by creating a system of their own laws that would keep people from violating God's command.

William Barclay tells us that the law permitted medical care only if a life was in danger. A woman giving birth could be assisted. If a well collapsed on someone, enough stone could be removed to determine if the person was alive, and if so he could be helped. At the same time, a fracture could not be set. A cut finger could be bandaged, but putting ointment on it was considered work and could not be done on the Sabbath.[1] Obviously the man with the withered hand was not in a life-or-death situation, so healing him on the Sabbath was a violation of the laws intended to keep the Sabbath holy.

It is impossible to miss Jesus' response to their lack of compassion toward the man with the handicap. He was angry at the hardness of their hearts, a hardness that preferred ritual and tradition over the healing of an innocent man. This same hardness exists in some churches today.

Caught early enough, heart disease can be reversed with treatment, proper diet, and exercise. Unfortunately, sometimes heart disease is not discovered until it is so far advanced that nothing can be done. By the time it is discovered, the only thing medicine can do is help the patient remain as comfortable as possible until he or she dies. This chapter will address what happens in a church whose heart has grown hard.

The Dead Church

We usually talk about healthy and nonhealthy churches, or growing and plateaued churches. I suppose it's not politically correct to talk about dead churches, but one of John's letters in Revelation 3 went to the church at Sardis. In that letter, God said, "I know your works, that you have a name that you are alive, but you are dead" (v. 1). This church had all the outward appearances of being a church, but God was not fooled and he did not hesitate in telling them they were dead.

What are the signs of a dead church? Read these sobering words from John MacArthur Jr.:

A church is in danger when it is content to rest on its past laurels, when it is more concerned with liturgical forms than spiritual reality, when it focuses on curing social ills rather than changing people's hearts through preaching the life-giving gospel of Jesus Christ, when it is more concerned with material than spiritual things, when it is more concerned with what men think that what God said, when it is more enamored with doctrinal creeds and systems of theology than with the Word of God, or when it loses its conviction that every word of the Bible is the word of God himself. No matter what its attendance, no matter how impressive its buildings, no matter what its status in the community, such a church, having denied the only source of spiritual life, is dead.[2]

As much as 80 percent of the churches in America are plateaued or declining, and some of them fit MacArthur's description. These churches may continue to have a presence in the community, but for all intents and purposes, these churches have already died from hardened hearts. Many of them will remain for decades—as long as a few faithful people attend and provide the financial resources to keep the doors open—but the Spirit of God has long departed. Whenever the spirit leaves the body, the body is dead, regardless of how long it remains on life support.

Anytime a church is more interested in maintaining its traditions and rituals than in fulfilling its God-given mission, that church is dead. Such churches point to a glorious past, but they cannot present a current vision for ministry. Many will have large pictures hanging on their walls showing hundreds of people attending an event in the church in the forties and fifties, but they cannot tell you the last time anyone was baptized.

What Do We Do with Dead Churches?

Some churches do not want to be healthy and enjoy a purposeful ministry, and some are so unhealthy that they cannot recover. I have had churches explain to me they did not want to do anything that might disrupt the fellowship they enjoyed with their longtime friends. If their church died as a result, at least they would all go down together. In other churches, the controllers ran the church for their benefit and no one was willing to challenge them. Both of these situations demonstrate unhealthiness within the body of Christ. However, you can't help someone who doesn't want to be helped, and the same thing is true of churches. The only thing that can be done in such churches is to allow them to continue down the path they are on until the only person left turns out the lights.

What we don't want to do is to artificially prop up such churches with financial assistance or expend resources that are needed elsewhere to try to help a church that really doesn't want to be helped. We also do not want to burn out good pastoral leadership in an effort to try to turn such churches around. Too many good pastors have burned out and left the ministry after doing everything possible to help turn around a church that didn't want to be turned around. Recently, I spoke with yet another pastor who was leaving the ministry because he burned out trying to help revive a church that had died years earlier. The good news is I believe he'll be back in the ministry within a few months after he and his wife have a time to heal. Unfortunately, some never return to ministry.

You may have heard the expression, "Whipping a dead horse won't make it run any faster." The same is true of a church. A dead church is dead even if it has money in the bank and people in the pews. Such churches may appear healthy on the outside, but inside they are filled with a disease that will prove to be terminal.

There must be few things more difficult for a doctor than having to tell a patient that nothing else can be done. A few years ago I was with a relative who received such news from his doctor. After two years of tests and treatments, they finally found the real cause of his problems, and by then it was too late for any effective treatment. The doctor struggled as he explained the diagnosis and the lack of treatment options. This was not news he wanted to give to anyone, and his sense of helplessness was obvious.

Just as it was painful for that doctor to deliver his report, it pains me to say that there may come a time when denominational and judicatory leadership can do nothing more for a church. Perhaps the best thing that can be done for such churches is to help them find dignity in their last days by becoming a legacy church as discussed in chapter 3. There is much more dignity in a church turning over its assets to another church or to the denomination than in continuing to dwindle away their resources on something that has no life. Such an unselfish act would be a great example of stewardship and would allow the church to close its doors with a sense of accomplishment rather than feeling like a failure because it could no longer remain open.

Denominations could assist such churches through their final days by providing them with pastors who could serve their churches much as a hospice chaplain. They could lead their churches in the decisions they need to make as they conclude their service to their communities. Depending on the polity of the denomination, decisions must made about what to do with the property and other assets of the church, but more important are the decisions about how to properly recognize and celebrate the positive ministry the church has provided to its community through the years. Regardless of the current condition of the church, lives have doubtlessly been impacted because that church existed. Perhaps thousands of people found faith in Christ through that church or families were restored because of that church's ministries. Young and old people alike found hope and a reason to go on because this church ministered to them in times of distress. There is much to celebrate, and it is important to recognize those accomplishments before the church closes its doors for the last time.

It will take a special pastor to be able to lead a church through this final transition. The last thing a church preparing to close its doors needs is a pastor who comes in with a checklist of things to accomplish. Rather, the church needs someone who has a genuine love for people, who understands the pain they are feeling as they begin the process, and who can lead them with grace, dignity, and patience. Judicatories would do well to provide specific training for a select group of ministers who would serve legacy churches.

Summary

Not every unhealthy church will survive, nor should we expect them to. Sometimes the spiritual disease is so advanced there is nothing that can be done. It is a mistake to keep such churches alive on life support. Such efforts will use up valuable and increasingly limited resources that could be better used elsewhere. The best thing for such churches is to leave their resources as a legacy for others to build upon. Such decisions should be applauded, and specially trained clergy should be provided to help churches through that transition.

Epilogue to Part 1

How did we ever get to the place where a church was nothing more than a one-and-a-half-hour service on a single day of the week at a specific location? I assure you, in Jesus' eyes, the Church is much more than that! He doesn't limit His Church to a building, a location, or a timeframe.[1]

—Neil Cole

I LOVE THE CHURCH. For the past three decades I have dedicated my life to leading the church, first as a pastor for twenty years and then as a judicatory leader for the past ten years. I have done so because I believe that the church is the one institution that offers genuine hope to hurting people. Government has its role, as do various service and charity organizations, but there is no other institution on earth that can offer people what the church offers. Unfortunately, the church often fails to offer such hope, and the evidence is all around us.

Marriages, both within and outside the church, continue to fail at astonishing rates. We are witnesses to a spiraling increase in drug and alcohol abuse, violence, STDs, crime, and sexual immorality of all types. At the same time, we are seeing an increase in spiritual things. Unfortunately, many spiritual pursuits bypass the church and take people down darker and darker paths that lead further away from the one true God.

A very talkative young server at a restaurant where my wife and I were dining learned I was a minister. Her next words were "I need God and don't know how to find him." She was unmarried with three children and living in a shelter for abused women and children. In a community filled with hundreds of churches, she did not know how to experience God in a life-changing way. No one had ever explained how God could come into her life and change it forever. The church failed her and millions of others like her.

According to Thom Rainer, one survey found that less than 15 percent of Christians had shared their faith with anyone in the previous year.[2] The Southern Baptist Convention is often considered one of the more evangelistic denominations, and yet they reported that in 2008 they baptized the lowest number of people since 1987. This was the fourth year in a row that they reported declining baptisms.[3]

The gospel is to be shared, but the church is keeping the good news to itself, and the result is that millions of people somehow know they need God in their lives but do not know where to find him.

We are not impacting our communities as God intended. If the majority of our churches closed tomorrow, how many people would notice the difference? One evening I was trying to find a rural church and stopped at three homes asking if they knew where the church was located. None of them knew, but when I finally found the church, it was less than three miles from each home. Would anyone living in those homes know if that church closed its doors?

Too many churches no longer know what they believe, making them incapable of speaking authoritatively about the many evils in the world. We often fail to extend grace even to our fellow believers, so we should not be surprised that the unchurched world does not expect to receive grace from the church. We have lost our sense of purpose as few churches clearly understand their mission, much less have any ownership of a personal vision for the fulfillment of that mission. Our churches are filled with baby Christians who need to be fed milk and not meat due to their immaturity. One of the reasons for all the shortcomings we've identified in our churches is that our denominations and seminaries have failed to produce the leaders we need to successfully minister in the twenty-first century.

These failures make the first part of this book extremely difficult to write for a couple of reasons. One is the knowledge that the church is living far below its potential, resulting in our inability to significantly impact people's lives for good. The second reason is that my own personal ministry has not measured up to what it could have been. I too have often failed to provide the pastoral leadership that churches deserved. Looking back over three decades of ministry I cannot help but be aware of the many times I could have done better. It hurts me to see my failures, but as I mentioned in the opening paragraph of this chapter, the church offers hope to hurting people. I grieve, but not as one without hope.

The final chapter of the church has not been written. The book of Acts is a historical account of the first-century church. It ends in chapter 28 with Paul's imprisonment in Rome, but I would argue that chapter 29 is still being written, describing the continuing work of the church through the present. As long as it is still being written there is hope that the church can recover its purpose and heart for ministry. Yes, the church has a serious disease preventing it from fulfilling its mission, but there is a cure. That cure begins by asking the tough questions that many churches avoid.

part 2
The Cure

8
Ask the Tough Questions

A significant measure of the health of the congregation is not where it stands in moments of comfort and ease, but rather, where it stands at times of challenge and crisis.[1]
—Peter L. Stenke

I CONCLUDED chapter 6 with one of the key questions every church must ask itself: who are we here for? The importance of this question cannot be overemphasized because the answer will impact everything a church does. If a church exists primarily for the benefit of its members, then its budgeting and programming will reflect that. The opposite is also true. If the church determines that it exists primarily for the benefit of the people who are not members (the position I take) then the budget and programming should reflect that. Perhaps the best way to answer the original question is to look at your current budget and programming. For most churches, both of these will heavily lean to the benefit of the members. Any money or programming for reaching out to the unchurched or making an impact on the community is an afterthought for many congregations. Show me your budget and your church calendar, and I will tell you what your vision for ministry is.

Jesus was repeatedly chastised for spending time with sinners and the unclean of the community. He responded, "Those who are well have no need of a physician, but those who are sick. But go and learn what this means: 'I desire mercy and not sacrifice.' For I did not come to call the righteous, but sinners, to repentance" (Matt. 9:12-13). Notice who was doing the chastising. It was always the religious leaders. They couldn't understand why this teacher wasn't content to spend his time with them rather than with the sinners. It seems like things haven't changed much in two thousand years.

I notice something else as well. Jesus constantly went to the people rather than setting up shop somewhere and hoping somebody would wander in off the street. He went to where the people were, accepted them where they were in their lives, and ministered to the needs they had. Neil Cole insists, "If you want to win this world to Christ, you are going to have to sit in the smoking section."[2] We avoid such sections, and as a result, we often avoid the people who sit in those sections. We don't want anyone to question our character, so we avoid the questionable people and places where they gather. We prefer to gather in our holy huddles in our safe places and minister to one another. Maybe—just maybe—we should follow Jesus' example and go where lost people are. The church is the one institution that exists for the benefit of its nonmembers, and we will only have the opportunity to impact their lives if we are spending our time with them.

Let's be clear. Little evangelistic ministry happens within the four walls of our churches. The Bible teaches us that we are not to forsake assembling together, but the purpose for such gathering is for worship, celebration, and instruction so each of us will be prepared to go out into the world Monday through Saturday to minister to those with whom we come into contact. Every Sunday when you leave your place of worship, you enter your mission field and it is your responsibility to offer Christ to the ones you meet in that mission field.

I realize that it is safer to minister to one another within the confines of our sanctuaries. Think about that word "sanctuary" for a minute. One of the definitions of a sanctuary is "a place of refuge and safety."[3] Too many of us prefer the safety of our sanctuaries over the risk of doing outreach ministry.

There is a great scene in the movie *Sister Act* where Whoopi Goldberg's character wants the nuns to leave the safety of their convent and go into a very dangerous neighborhood that surrounds them. The mother superior absolutely forbids it because it would be too dangerous, but she is overruled by the priest. As the nuns venture out into the neighborhood they find numerous ways to influence the people they encounter, and the people respond by filling up the sanctuary on the following Sundays. What happened in the movie may not happen to you, but regardless of whether or not people respond by coming to our churches, there is no doubt that the church is called to be actively involved in the community. We cannot influence people if we are not among the people, and it is the hurting and the lost that we have been commanded to reach.

Who are we here for? I pray that your church answers that question by stating that it exists to serve the people in their surrounding community who do not yet have a personal relationship with God through Jesus Christ. If so, then you are ready for the second tough question.

Is What We Are Doing Worth the Life of the Son of God?

I got cold chills the first time I heard someone ask this question. Because I am sometimes not very tactful, I often rephrase this question to ask, "Did Jesus really die for *this*?" When I look at much of what the church spends its time addressing, I have trouble believing that the Son of God left the splendor of heaven to die on a wooden cross so the church could continue dealing with trifles. As a judicatory leader I've seen some of the most foolish things become the basis for Christian fellowship. Of course, the ones arguing would disagree with my opinion that the issues are trivial, but it is hard for me to believe God is really that interested in the color of our carpet or the brand of coffee we serve after the worship service.

Think back to your last church business meeting. How much of that meeting was devoted to vital issues that could impact the lives of real people, and how much of it addressed trivial issues that will be meaningless within five years? Ask the same question of the last church committee meeting you attended. Some time ago I sat in a deacon meeting at the request of the pastor and deacons. The pastor gave a report of how many times he had visited members of the church since their last meeting a month prior, the number of telephone contacts he had with people, and the number of times he visited members in the hospital. There is nothing wrong with any of these, but at no time in this meeting was any time spent planning for the future. Neither the pastor nor any lay leader ever addressed the future or spoke about how the church could fulfill its vision, probably because the church has no vision for future ministry. Everything they did that evening was looking back at how well the pastor had ministered to the congregation, and if a sufficient number of contacts with church members were made, it was considered a successful month. Is this why Jesus Christ died on the cross, so pastors can report on how many times they checked in with the saints? Did Christ have to die so churches could argue over whether to get hymnals with red covers or blue ones?

If a pastor challenges people to become more involved in ministry activities, many of them would respond that they are already very busy attending church functions and engaged in various committee and board work. Many would correctly argue they don't have time to add anything else to their schedules. This is where the question becomes very important. Is what you are currently doing worth the life of the Son of God, or could that time and effort be better used in some other activity? I challenge church leaders to look at everything that is currently being done in their churches and measure it against this question. If the activity is not producing results worthy of the sacrifice of Jesus Christ, then it may be time to set aside that activity for one that will make a significant difference in people's lives. Let's not waste the time and gifts of people in mundane tasks that really no longer matter. Instead, let's free up people's time and challenge them to become involved in ministries that are truly worthy of the death of God's Son.

Who Is Jesus to You?

Perhaps the most important exchange Jesus had with his disciples occurred in Matthew 16:13-17 when he asked, "Who do men

139

say that I, the Son of Man, am?" When the disciples responded with various answers, Christ made the question more personal: "But who do you say that I am?" For a few moments I imagine it got real quiet until Peter gave his famous answer that Jesus was "the Christ, the Son of the living God."

This is the question that each person and each church must answer for themselves. The individual's answer will determine his or her relationship with Christ, and the church's answer will determine the kind of church it will be. A church that sees Christ as passive and indifferent to things will become much the same. A church that believes Jesus Christ conquered death, now has all authority, and is the truth, the life, and the only way by which we come to the Father (see John 14:6) will be bold in its witness and in its ministry to the surrounding community. The problem is that too many churches say they believe these things, but their actions do not support their words.

Before my wife and I became Christians I would occasionally ask her these questions. "We both believe in heaven, don't we?" She would answer that we do. "We both believe in hell, don't we?" Again, she would answer in the affirmative. I would then ask, "Why then do we live like we want to go to hell?" For a long time neither of us could answer that question because we didn't like where the answer was going to take us. It was not a matter of not knowing. We had both been raised in churches as children and teenagers. We knew there was a God, and we both knew enough about him to be miserable about the lives we were living. But, and it is a big but, we didn't want to change our lifestyles, which we knew we would have to do if we truly invited Jesus into our lives.

Let me be very frank here. There is something seriously wrong with churches that call themselves conservative or evangelical and are not focusing on reaching unchurched people for Jesus Christ. If your church claims to believe in heaven and hell and that Jesus

Christ is the only way a person can enter into a personal relationship with God, then it should be doing everything it can to get that message out to as many people as possible. The biblical heaven and hell are both eternal places, and every person who has ever lived will, if we truly believe the Bible, spend eternity in one or the other. Your parents, your grandparents, your children, your coworkers, your neighbor, your barber—every person you know, including you, will spend eternity in either heaven or hell. You determine which of these two destinations will be yours based on what you do with Jesus Christ now, in this life. There is absolutely nothing that your church can do that is more important than getting that word out to every person within your sphere of influence, if you truly believe what the Bible says. Yet, many churches that call themselves conservative and evangelical argue to the last breath that they believe in the Word of God, while cobwebs grow in their baptisteries and pews.

Why is this? It's the same problem I had in my personal life. I knew the right things to say, but I didn't want to change my lifestyle. Many churches have become comfortable in their ruts. They are satisfied with the number of people they have, they enjoy their holy huddle on Sunday morning, and they don't want to change.

It is God's will to reach everyone with the gospel, so why don't our churches reach them? It comes down to unwillingness to make the necessary changes for reaching unchurched people. If your church could reach new people by doing what it has always done, it would already be reaching them, wouldn't it? Obviously something has to change, but until we love people as much as Jesus does, many of our churches are not going to change.

Who do you really believe Jesus is? How will you prove it? As I said before, you must back up what you say with actions. Show me your budget and your calendar, and I can tell you your church's view of Jesus.

Do You Love People as Much as Jesus Does?

I probably know how most churches will answer, so I'll ask another question. Who are the people you love?

Congregations often tell me their church is the friendliest church in town. In fact, I have yet to meet the second-friendliest church in any community! However, my experience from visiting in hundreds of churches is that many of them are very friendly to one another, but not always to strangers. They are very friendly to their brothers and sisters in the faith, but they can freeze out an outsider, especially if that person is different from them.

Part of the mission of the church, as discussed earlier, is to fulfill the Great Commandment, which includes the command to love our neighbor as we love ourselves. On the night he was betrayed, Jesus took a basin of water and washed the feet of his disciples. He even washed the feet of Judas, who would betray him before the night was over. If we believe Jesus was omniscient, we have to also believe he knew that Judas was the one who would betray him, but it didn't matter. Even on this night, Jesus extended God's grace to the one who would soon turn him over to be killed. The church today is called to love people that are a lot more like Judas than Jesus.[4] Does your church love such people, and if so, how is that love demonstrated?

The apostle John had very strong words for anyone who claimed he loved God but did not love his fellow man (1 John 4:20-21), and James insisted that a Christian's faith would always be demonstrated by his actions (James 2:14-20). If we claim to love others as Christ does, then that love must be demonstrated through our actions. So, I ask again, how is your church demonstrating its love for people?

Are members of your church developing relationships with people outside of the church? Several years ago our church conducted an "Invite a Friend Day." We followed the plan exactly as it had been developed, and on Friend Sunday we had exactly the same attendance we always did. As I began to ask why no one brought a friend, we found out that none of us had any unchurched friends. One woman told me she could not remember a time she was not a Christian and involved in church, and she had no friends who were not Christians. We agreed this was not the way Christians should live, so many of us began to intentionally build relationships with non-Christians. The next year we conducted Friend Day again, and this time we not only saw an increase in attendance but within a few months saw some new people give their lives to Christ.

You may think your church is the friendliest church in town, but the fact is unchurched people are not looking for a "friendly church" where the people are nice and polite but are not open to true friendship with visitors and seekers. They are looking for friends. They are lonely and want to be part of a community. I am convinced that if Christians offer genuine community, people will get involved in the church and, more importantly, will begin to seriously consider the claims of Jesus Christ.

People matter to God, and because they matter to God they should matter to God's people. God gave his Son so people could have a personal relationship with him. Regardless of a person's particular sins, he or she is someone for whom Jesus Christ gave his life. People are created in the image of God, which makes them worthy of our respect. We don't have to approve of the choices they have made in their lives. However, if we claim to love God, we had better love those who have been created in the image of God or the faith we claim to have is nothing more than words. In case you didn't know, God didn't like some of the choices you and I made in our lives either. That didn't keep him from reaching down into our lives and drawing us to him. God probably used someone who was willing to overlook those sinful choices to introduce us to his love and offer of forgiveness. I can thank a number of Christian men with whom I worked who loved me when I wasn't very lovable and shared the love of God with me at a time when I desperately needed to hear of that love. Who are the people you are loving to God today?

Who are the people you are praying for? Just prior to his betrayal, Jesus prayed for his disciples and for those who follow after them. That would be you and me. Jesus knew his death was only a matter of hours away, and yet he took time to pray for us. It's another demonstration of his love for us. Who are the people you love so much that you pray for them every day? It's not too hard to pray for family members every day, but it's another story when we start praying for people who do not like us very much.

A pastor was often confronted by a parishioner who complained about nearly everything the pastor and his family did. The week after one brutal encounter, the pastor was planning on preaching on love when God began to challenge him about his attitudes toward this church member. The pastor stopped his sermon preparation long enough to pray for this individual and his family. Immediately after the service, the pastor went directly to the individual and told him how much he appreciated his presence there that day. Throughout the year, the pastor seldom failed to pray God's blessings on this man and his family. At the end of that year, he visited this man's wife in the hospital, and during that visit she told him how much her husband now respected this pastor.[5] Could you pray for those who falsely accuse you and say all matter of evil against you? We can do that only if we love people as Christ does.

What Price Are You Willing to Pay?

If a person has a heart attack or discovers he or she has some type of heart disease, he or she must make lifestyle changes. Quite often the individual has to make changes in diet, exercise, rest, and activities. Occasionally, the individual is unwilling to make those changes. Doctors can do little at that point. Only the people who genuinely want improved health are willing to make the necessary changes. The same is true for churches.

Most plateaued and declining churches know very well they are in trouble. The very fact that a church is plateaued or declining is proof enough that something has to change. They know they are not healthy, but many of them are obviously unwilling to make the needed changes. Instead, they prefer to remember the good old days and play church games. Robert Nash describes one popular game.

We play a little game each week in church called "Let's Pretend." We pretend that people want the same things from church in the 1990s that they wanted in the 1950s. We pretend that the majority of Americans are churchgoing Christians who believe in the God of the Bible and who order their lives to reflect this reality. We pretend that the spirituality of Americans in the 1990s is enhanced by a decades-old diet of practical faith, old-time religion, revivals, and personal "quiet time." We pretend that the church is still the center of community life and that people will come back to church "when they get their lives straightened out."[6]

We're still playing this popular game in the twenty-first century. The problem is that Christian beliefs and values no longer dominate the thinking of most Americans, even many who call themselves Christians. Another problem is that people are not going to return to the church because they never left the church. In fact, they have never been a part of the church so they have nothing to return to. They may find a time in their lives when they begin seeking God, but that doesn't mean they are going to look for him in the church. Churches play this game because it's easier to say these things than to do the hard work of looking at ourselves and trying to understand how the church has failed so badly in taking God to a confused and hurting world.

Another popular game is to blame the pastor. Some churches operate like a professional sports team. If the team isn't winning, replace the coach. If the church isn't growing, replace the pastor. Many churches still believe if they could just find the right pastor, everything would be all right. The church would grow, finances would increase, the youth department would flourish, and everything would be great. These churches never find such a person, but that doesn't stop them from looking every two or three years. It's much easier to look for a new pastor than to look at their own failings.

One game some churches play is to question the spiritual depth of churches that are growing. Willow Creek Community Church in South Barrington, Illinois, is a favorite target of such criticism as the critics rail against the seeker services the church offers each weekend to nearly twenty thousand people. The critics seldom note the midweek services for Christians and the many discipleship programs the church offers to promote spiritual growth among believers.

Such criticism isn't limited to only the megachurches like Willow Creek. I hear the same criticism from smaller, established churches when a new community church comes into the area and their attendance quickly surpasses the older churches. Leaders of those smaller churches often complain that these new churches are reaching people because they compromise the message of the gospel or because these churches are "the place in town to be seen." The small church leaders console themselves by trying to convince themselves and others that they are part of the faithful remnant, while these fast-growing churches have somehow compromised the message in order to attract people. Perhaps this is true for some churches, but it certainly isn't true of the majority of them. The critics might be surprised at the conservative theology many of these churches proclaim.

The bottom line is that plateaued or dying churches will have to change in order to turn things around, and many of them are not willing to pay the price for such change. Is your congregation willing to pay the price of change? More importantly, are *you* willing to pay the price?

Summary

When a person is diagnosed with a heart problem, that person often has to make some major lifestyle decisions. None of these changes are easy or enjoyable to make, but they are necessary to regain health. The same thing is true of a church. Changes must be made, and the first step is to ask the tough questions addressed in this chapter. Asking the questions isn't that difficult; providing honest answers is the difficult part. In my experience, churches often give the best-sounding answer whether or not that answer is true about them. However, a church shouldn't lie about its heart problem, just as an individual shouldn't lie to his or her doctor. Nothing changes if we continue to act like everything is as it should be, and if nothing changes, a church cannot be restored to health and become an effective witness to its community.

9

Pursue Congregational Health

As a system, a congregation influences its
own health. By taking responsible action,
it shapes its destiny.[1]

—Peter L. Steinke

A FRIEND OF MINE smoked cigarettes for many years. Later in life he developed a number of health problems because of his smoking. Not only did he have heart bypass surgery, but he also had a number of surgeries to bypass arteries in his legs. Despite these surgeries and the knowledge that his smoking was the primary cause of his health problems, he continued to smoke. Finally, the doctor told him in no uncertain terms that there was little more medically that could be done for him if he did not stop smoking immediately. When he finally came to terms with what his actions were doing to him, he stopped smoking immediately. He told me he didn't want to stop; he enjoyed smoking and had smoked since he was a young boy. However, he also enjoyed life and finally realized he had the power to impact not only the length of his life but the quality of his life as well. I have no doubt in my mind that his stopping smoking added several years to his life.

The health of your church is determined by the actions of the leadership and congregation. God has already revealed that he desires the church to be an unstoppable force in the world (see Matt. 16:18). Whether or not it is depends on the people who make up the church. Your church is what it is today because of decisions it made years ago, and the future of your church will be determined by the decisions you make today. If you want it to be the force God imagined, you must take the necessary steps to make that happen, and one of those steps to ensure that your church remains healthy. One way of ensuring health is to stop the spread of "viruses" in the church.

Peter Steinke identifies four of those viruses that are often found in unhealthy churches. They are secrets and gossip, accusations, lies, and triangulation.[2] Let's briefly look at each of these.

Secrets and Gossip

A pastor began his ministry in a new church. In less than six weeks he was confronted with the fact that a staff member was having an inappropriate relationship with a member of the church. The staff member was confronted, admitted his failure, repented, and sought counseling. This was not the first time this staff member had an affair with a member of the church, but few people knew of the previous situation. The new pastor soon learned this wasn't the only secret this church had. According to him, this church had many secrets and was a very unhealthy place to serve. He left within the first year.

No organization is any healthier than the secrets it keeps. Because secrecy is such a serious issue in churches, it is essential that churches not encourage secret-keeping.[3] Problems do not go away by ignoring them. In fact, ignoring them usually allows them to grow larger. Secrets should be brought into the open as quickly as possible to keep them from damaging the church. Rumors and gossip must be stopped immediately to keep them from spreading.

I was once asked to speak to a church that was embroiled in a major conflict. In my message that morning, I directly addressed the underlying issue that brought about the conflict. I asked the rhetorical question, what should the congregation do about the issue, and I told them the first thing that needed to happen was that some of them needed to go home and unplug their telephones. It was time to stop the rumors and the backbiting that had been going on for several months. Innocent people had been hurt; a number of people had left the church; further gossip and whispering about this issue was only going to continue the unhealthy atmosphere that existed in the church. It was time to put this behind them, stop dwelling on what had happened, and move forward to become healthy again.

Accusations

When we accuse, we are pointing fingers and blaming people for alleged failures. Often, accusations are made without having all the facts. We hear a rumor about someone's behavior and assume it is true without checking it out for ourselves. Have you ever noticed this is especially easy if the rumor is about someone we don't especially care for anyway?

One pastor was asked by a leader in the church to confront a member about a supposed moral failure in her life. The pastor asked the basis of the concern, and the leader said that he had been told that someone read something on Facebook that indicated this person might be living in sin. There was insufficient evidence for confrontation. *Someone* read *something* that *indicated* there *might* be a problem! Fortunately, the pastor was wise enough to refuse this leader's request, and when the leader shared his concern with the church board, it supported the pastor's decision. A virus was stopped before it had a chance to spread. Unfortunately, this doesn't always happen.

Accusations often come from unidentified sources. Someone will come with a complaint supposedly representing a number of people. Often, that large number of people will only be the person's spouse and perhaps one other couple. Ask the person bringing the accusation to identify the people he or she represents or state your willingness to go with them to hear the concerns of these other people firsthand. Do not act on anonymous complaints or accusations, and make your congregation aware of this policy. I refuse to even read a note or email if it does not have a signature attached to it. I look for the signature first, and if there isn't one, I don't bother to read the note. It goes directly into the trash.

Once, a leader wanted his church to leave the denomination of which it had always been a part. He based his desire on one particular issue he had with the denomination. I was invited to address the issue in his church. He spoke first, listing all the reasons why the church needed to leave. I addressed his concerns and noted that most of them were based upon half-truths, a misunderstanding of where the denomination stood on the issue, and a complete disregard for the actions that were being taken to address the issue. He never lied to the church, but the church was deceived by his arguments because they were not based upon facts. He had failed to do his homework and relied on the opinions of others who, in many cases, were not even members of that denomination. The next week, after the church's business meeting, he called to let me know the church voted to leave the denomination. I recently spoke to a former pastor of that church who still has contact with some members. He told me the church continues to struggle and is very unhealthy.

Lies

It's a shame that lying even has to be addressed as a virus in churches, but unfortunately, some Christian people will do anything to promote their opinion. No organization can be healthy if it is continually fed a diet of lies and deception. Persons telling blatant lies should be challenged immediately about their actions.

A pastor recently told me of a church member who opposed a certain project in the church and tried to get people to vote against it by telling them things about the project that were not true. When he confronted her about her actions, she resigned her positions in the church and left the church. These types of actions lead to confusion and frustration among church members and can impact the future ministry of the church.

Triangulation

Triangulation is a situation in which one party gets caught in the middle of a conflict between two other parties. Offended parties want support. People on both sides of a disagreement try to rally support from others. They reveal secrets and spread rumors and lies. The pastor is an especially inviting target for those seeking to bring other people into their camp. He or she would be proof positive that their side of the issue is correct.

In one church, two camps were at odds. One side believed the accusations that were being made, while the other side blamed the accusers of spreading lies. Several years have passed, and I doubt either side has changed its opinion. The matter has been dropped, and on the surface things seem back to normal as the congregation has moved on with new leadership. However, it is highly likely that in a future contest these two sides will quickly reunite. You'll notice I didn't say the matter was resolved; it was merely dropped, and another issue will probably bring everything back to the surface again. Even though the church has moved on, it never addressed the viruses that had brought the previous disease, and the church remains unhealthy as a result.

It Begins with the Leaders

It is essential that leaders model healthy attitudes and behaviors. Jonathan Falwell assumed the pastorate of Thomas Road Baptist Church when his father, Jerry Falwell, passed away. Since becoming the pastor, the church has experienced amazing growth due to the exciting ministries it has developed. Among these ministries there are a number of adult Bible communities designed to minister to and spiritually develop their new members. One of the challenges in starting so many new ministries is developing leaders to lead them. No organization, including churches, will be any healthier than the people who lead it. Falwell insists, "To develop a healthy church, you must develop healthy leaders who develop healthy members."[4]

If the leaders of the church are not spiritually and emotionally healthy, we cannot expect the church to be. Likewise, if the leaders of the church are not growing in spiritual and emotional health, the congregation is unlikely to grow. This requires leaders to spend time in the Scriptures, in prayer, and in assessment of their personal growth. As they continue their own spiritual journey, they will be able to lead others in their journey as well.

Healthy leaders leading healthy churches brings a passion to ministry.[5] One of the things I often notice in plateaued and declining churches is the lack of passion found in either the worship services or the leaders of the congregation. After visiting with such churches or their leaders, I feel exhausted, as if all of the energy has been sucked out of me. If I can sense a lack of passion, so can visitors, and this is a primary reason why they don't return.

If you are a leader in your church, you must take personal responsibility for your spiritual, emotional, and physical health. This will require you to spend time in the Scriptures, in prayer, and in self-care. On the surface, this sounds simple enough. After all, shouldn't pastors be spending time in prayer and Bible study? Yes, but those of us who have been in ministry a while know that most churches do not judge a pastor's worth by the amount of time he or she spends alone with God. We receive our accolades for the work we are doing. Many of us have learned that the ones who evaluate our efforts look at what we are doing, not at our personal spiritual development. Leaders who are hungry for human approval will spend their time doing things that earn this approval, and, sad to say, there are too many such leaders.

To be quite honest, one in the ministry for any length of time soon learns that he or she can do an adequate job without doing much more than giving God lip service. One can take the right courses, buy the right books, learn the right techniques, and satisfy just about every demand anyone in the church makes. The only one we won't satisfy is the spirit within each of us that is hungry for more of God. We know, whether anyone else does or not, that we are running on empty and offering clichés because we have nothing fresh to give.

How refreshing it would be if churches told their pastors they needed to spend less time in the church office and more time alone with God. Not only would it be refreshing, but it would bring much-needed health to the congregation. The pastor would have a fresh word from God instead of comments from the margins of his or her seminary class notes. He or she would be leading out of a fresh experience with God. There would be a new dynamic in the worship services and even in board and committee meetings.

Attributes of Healthy Churches

I am indebted to Ron Blake for the following information on the attributes of healthy churches. Blake was one of the contributors to *The Pastor's Guide to Effective Ministry,* and in his chapter he identified some of the attributes of healthy churches. I would encourage the reader to read this entire book and especially the chapter from which some of this material originated. Blake lists seven characteristics of healthy churches, which we will briefly examine.[6]

1. Healthy churches help everyone discover a sense of purpose. In many churches the Pareto Principle is alive and well; 20 percent of the people do 80 percent of the work. Healthy churches believe and teach that every believer has a God-given purpose and the work of the church will be successful when everyone is involved in ministry. People are not allowed to sit on the sidelines but are encouraged to identify their spiritual gift mix and are challenged to use those gifts in serving others. Opportunities for ministry are provided so there is a place for everyone to serve. Churches that have such expectations and offer ministry opportunities to their members often see a much higher percentage of people involved in ministry.

These churches are attractive to Christians and non-Christians alike. Not only do they help people discover a reason for living beyond themselves, but healthy churches model a sense of purpose in their own ministries. One can call that a sense of vision or a sense of purpose, but these churches know what they believe and where they are going, and they challenge others to join them on that journey.[7] That is much more attractive than a church that is just drifting along hoping something good will happen someday.

2. Healthy churches create a place of belonging for people. Americans are among the loneliest people in the world. Many of us live next door to people we don't know and who do not know us. We isolate ourselves in office cubicles during the day, on back decks surrounded by privacy fences during the evening, and in our living rooms watching television at night. Interaction with others is often limited to emails and text messages. Churches that offer a sense of community to people in the twenty-first century will grow. As stated earlier, people are not looking for a friendly church as much as they are looking for a church where they can make some friends. Healthy churches offer people a place to belong and know that others genuinely care for them.

3. Healthy churches intentionally create trust among its members. N. Graham Standish believes "a church can be healthy without a vision, but it cannot be healthy without trust."[8] I'm not sure I agree that a church can be healthy without a vision, but I certainly do agree that it cannot be healthy without trust. It is probably not a stretch to state that most of the plateaued and declining churches are low-trust churches, and that is one reason they are declining. It's why these churches insist that every decision be run past numerous boards and committees and then brought to a business meeting for final approval. The people do not trust the leadership nor do they trust one another. In such churches it is impossible to create a true sense of community because trust is foundational for any relationship.

Healthy churches intentionally seek ways to develop trust. They find ways to work together. When mistakes are made and people fail in some area, they are quick to encourage and lift up rather than condemn. One of the things I was most thankful for in the church I served was that they allowed me to make mistakes as their pastor. Believe me, they got plenty of practice in extending grace toward me. This doesn't mean I wasn't held accountable, and there were times when church members challenged some of the mistakes I made, but the mistakes were never fatal. As a result, they trusted me and I trusted them. Healthy churches experience such trust.

4. *Healthy churches provide many opportunities for people to form relationships.* Healthy, growing churches provide numerous small-group opportunities in which people can develop relationships with others. Plateaued and declining churches usually have few opportunities for people to form relationships with other people. Such opportunities are often limited to worship services and existing small groups such as a Sunday school class or choir. Healthy churches consistently look for ways to start new small groups where people can be more comfortable. They understand that new people are reluctant to join existing groups, so new groups are regularly formed that new people can join together. The exciting thing is that churches can develop groups around any interest that people may have.

A small church recently began a new group focused on fishing. This group is led by a church member who loves to fish and has entered several fishing tournaments. If this group does well, the church plans to add new groups based on people's interests. The only factor that limits the number of groups a church can have is the leadership to run the groups.

Some traditionalists will complain that the midweek service should focus on prayer and Bible study, not on fishing or quilting. At this point let me again ask my Dr. Phil question: how is that working for you? If your church is like most, your midweek service, if you still have one, is by far the poorest attended service in your church. In each of these affinity groups, there is time spent in prayer and Bible study, but perhaps the most important thing happening in these groups is that Christians and non-Christians are brought together to develop friendships around common interests, and in these relationships there are opportunities for people to hear how Jesus Christ has changed lives.

5. *Healthy churches get as many people as possible involved in ministry.* Some churches complain that new people go out the back door almost as fast as they come through the front door. One of the ways to stop the bleeding is to get people involved in ministry. People in the twenty-first century want to feel they can make a difference, and if they are not given an opportunity to do so in your church, they will seek another place where their gifts and passions will be better appreciated and used.

The challenge for some churches is that new people are not always interested in joining a church. People today tend to not be concerned about maintaining membership in an organization, but they do want to be involved. Unhealthy churches have little, if anything, a nonmember can do. I often joke to workshop participants that in some churches you're not allowed to take out the garbage if you're not a member of the church. Healthy churches are less concerned about membership and more concerned with giving people opportunities to be involved in meaningful activities for which they are equipped. If your church is unwilling to do that, don't be surprised when your new people disappear.

6. *Healthy churches keep the mission and vision before the people.* Such churches never assume everyone remembers the mission and vision of the church, nor do they assume everyone has bought into them. Healthy churches consistently keep both the mission and vision of the church in front of the people and show them how they can be a part of fulfilling them. A leader cannot remind people of the vision too often. "Marketing and sales experts say that people generally need to hear an idea seven times before they will embrace

it and call it their own idea."[9] From my experience I would say the same is true for churches. Rick Warren insists that a church leader must remind the church of its vision every twenty-six days or many of them will forget.[10]

7. Healthy churches regularly train and equip their people for ministry. As Blake says, "Giving people something to do and then not providing them the necessary tools or equipment leads to frustration and high turnover."[11] It amazes me that the church seems to be the one organization that believes it can ask people to assume a responsibility and feel no need to train them how to best fulfill that responsibility. We ask someone to teach a Sunday school class, hand them a teacher's guide, and show them their room, and then wonder why they didn't do a better job of teaching and why they are not excited to teach the class the next year. If we are serious about expecting people to be involved in ministry, then we must be equally serious about training them so they can be successful in their efforts.

Pastors often complain to me about the lack of leaders in their churches. One of the reasons some churches have so few leaders is that they have done nothing to develop leaders. If we want a steady supply of leaders in our churches, we have to ensure there are people in the pipeline who are preparing to provide such leadership. If we wait until we need leaders to train them, it will be too late. We need to be consistently training leaders and then finding places where they can use their newfound knowledge and skills. Believe me, if you have a good leader, there will not be a problem finding that person a ministry in which he or she can serve. Healthy churches see the value in consistently training new leaders, so they are always prepared for any new thing God wants to do in their churches.

Pursuing Health

Now that we've noted some of the attributes of a healthy church, many readers are asking how their church can pursue health. I have dealt with this question in detail in *The Healthy Small Church*, so I won't duplicate that material here. The final chapter of that book provides diagnostic questions church leaders can use to examine thirteen different aspects of their churches, and I recommend doing such a diagnosis once a year. Just as our bodies benefit from having a yearly physical examination, the body of Christ will benefit from having an annual checkup. When you notice something is wrong in a specific area, address it. Help that aspect of your church return to health as quickly as possible and your entire church will benefit.

Healthy Churches Require Healthy Leaders

Remember, pastors and other leaders must model healthy behavior and attitudes. Stephen Macchia insists that "if a church is to be healthy and vital, it needs to be led by a pastor and leadership team who are themselves pursuing health in their personal lives and in their shared leadership capacity. Only then will a local church become the vibrant, healthy entity God intends."[12] Another person who has extensively studied church health is Peter Scazzero. He writes, "The overall health of any church or ministry depends primarily on the emotional and spiritual health of its leadership. In fact, the key to successful spiritual leadership has much more to do with the leader's internal life than with the leadership expertise, gifts, or experience."[13]

It would be impossible to fully address all the qualities of a healthy leader in this book. No list of such qualities would completely satisfy every reader anyway. However, there are some basics that would probably appear on every list. At the top of my list would be a personal relationship with Jesus Christ that is consistently developed through regular times of prayer, Bible study, meditation, and self-examination. Without such a relationship one might be a leader, but one cannot be a spiritual leader, and spiritual leadership is what we need most in today's church. We have plenty of CEO-type leaders in the church; we need men and women who have an ongoing relationship with Christ who are committed to growing deeper in that relationship with him.

Other attributes healthy church leaders must have are:

- Integrity
- Vision
- Humility
- Courage
- Patience
- A servant's heart
- A sense of call to the position

I'm sure you would add other qualities to this list, but the important thing to note is that none of these speak of a leader's gifts, abilities, or educational achievements. These are all internal attributes that reflect the leader's character. The more each of these are developed within the leader, the healthier that leader will be, and the healthier his or her church will be. If enough of these qualities are absent in the leader's life, the church will soon reflect that same dysfunction in its own life.

Summary

Just as individuals must decide to pursue healthy habits in their lives, so do churches. Good health doesn't just happen. Churches must take intentional steps to be healthy and continually monitor themselves to ensure that they remain that way. Healthy churches also require their leaders to be healthy, both pastoral and lay, and it is vital for such leadership to take the necessary actions to maintain good spiritual, physical, emotional, and mental health.

10
Pay the Price of Change

We must be the change we seek.[1]

—Gandhi

WE CLOSED chapter 8 by asking if your church, and you personally, are prepared to pay the price for change. There will certainly be a price to pay, but most people seem to be unwilling to pay it.

For much of my adult life I struggled with weight issues. In 2009, I set a goal to reduce my weight from 220 pounds to 180 pounds. For the first half of the year I was not successful. In fact, I gained an additional nine pounds! That summer I decided I needed to find a program that would help me achieve my goal and joined Weight Watchers. I also worked out at a local gym three or four days a week. By mid-March of 2010 I weighed 179 pounds—a loss of fifty pounds! My wife ate the same meals I did and also lost weight. As a result, she was able to go off all her high blood pressure medicine.

Weight Watchers gave me a structured program that was effective, but I had to work it. I had to track my points, eat the correct portions of food, and stop eating a lot of food I always enjoyed. As a judicatory minister I am invited to a lot of church potluck meals, and our churches have a lot of excellent cooks. I left before many of those meals began, and when I did stay for a church dinner, I was very selective about what I ate. I travel a lot leading workshops for various groups, and that meant I had to be very careful about what restaurants I chose and what I ordered. Ignoring desserts and fried food wasn't fun, but it was enjoyable watching the weight come off week after week when I attended the Weight Watchers' meetings. It was even more enjoyable the day I stepped on the scale and it registered 179 pounds. The most fun came when I bought a pair of new pants and found I had dropped two sizes. I achieved my goal, but I had to pay a price to do so.

If I was serious about wanting to change my life, I had to be willing to make changes. There were financial costs, emotional costs, and social costs involved in making this change, and for many years

I had been unwilling to pay the price. This refusal came despite knowing that my mother struggled with diabetes, which took most of her sight before she passed away, high blood pressure, and suffered a stroke that had a serious impact on her physical and mental health. In addition, my father had a triple-bypass heart surgery, and suffered complications years later while undergoing a second bypass operation. He never left the hospital. For years I fought high blood pressure and was taking four different medications to control it. My family history is not good when it comes to heart problems, which made my need to get control of my weight and blood pressure very important. Despite knowing the potential risks of not doing anything, for much of my life I was not willing to pay the price.

I assume most readers of this book are pastors and lay leaders of their churches. I encourage you to take a good, honest look at your church. How healthy is your church? Does it understand God's vision for its current ministry and is it seeking ways to fulfill that vision? What changes need to occur to help your church function as God intended? What exactly are you willing to do in order to help your church become healthy? Jesus taught the value of counting the cost before beginning something (see Luke 14:28-32), and that is what we must do before beginning any significant change in our churches.

Cost of Change

Change in Pastoral Leadership

John Maxwell tells the story of a lunch meeting he once had with an individual whose company purchased troubled hotels and resorts. This individual told Maxwell that when they bought one of these businesses, they always did two things: they trained the employees to provide better service and they fired the leader. Maxwell was amazed that they didn't first try to work with that leader to see how good of a leader he or she was. The individual replied that if he or she had been any good, the organization wouldn't have been in trouble and purchased by his company.[2]

This sounds extreme, but George Barna insists that "to turn around a church, *a new pastor must be brought in* to lead the revolution. Some churches probably have come back from the edge of extinction without a change in pastor. However, we did not find such a church. In every one of the churches we explored, a new pastor had to be brought in to create the climate and plans for a successful resurrection of the congregation."[3] I read Barna's comments soon after his book was published. It happened to be at a time when our church was not doing as well as I would have liked. We seemed to be stuck without any sense of direction. I had been there over a decade and was weary and out of fresh ideas. When I read Barna's words about a church needing a new pastor in order to turn things around, I thought maybe this was God's way of telling me it was time to resign and move to another place of ministry. Yet, I didn't sense God saying that. It then dawned on me that perhaps I could become a new pastor. Within a few weeks I preached a sermon to our congregation that included Barna's comments. Some assumed I was leading up to announcing my resignation. Instead, I told the congregation that with God's help I wanted to become the new pastor the church needed. Over the next few months I changed my style of preaching as well as some of the ways I approached ministry. As Gandhi advocated, I became the change I sought. As I changed, our church began to change as well.

Eventually, there came a time when I realized that the church did require new pastoral leadership. I had been there twenty years and began to understand the church needed new leadership with gifts different from mine. This was a very painful time for me. I had invested two decades of my life in that congregation. My parents and most of my friends were in that church.

It is unlikely there will be any significant change until pastors change or step aside to allow a new pastor to come in. I wonder how many pastors are willing to pay that price to see churches regain their health and begin a new life cycle. It is one thing to sing in church about our willingness to surrender all to Jesus, but are we willing to surrender our pastoral position if doing so would help our churches be healthier and have a greater impact for the kingdom of God?

Remaining at a church while introducing change often requires the pastor to straddle two roles: the traditional pastoral role many in the church expect, and the role of an agent of change, introducing new ways of doing ministry to the church.

> While the pastor is [sowing] the seeds of vision, the pastor is fulfilling well those ministries and responsibilities that are designed to keep the congregation small and effective at meeting member needs. Failure to do so will cause the pastor to lose credibility and reduce any future leverage for change. The pastor still functions as a chaplain: visiting, caring, and counseling. The pastor still attends the endless committee meetings that produce no growth and reinforce the power of the church bosses. The pastor fulfills all the expected roles required in highly dysfunctional congregations, realizing they are providing the future political capital to lead change.[4]

This time when a pastor is both chaplain and innovator can be very frustrating, and often takes three to five years. While the pastor is identifying future leaders to train and preparing them for ministry, he or she is expected to maintain the status quo. As Borden correctly states above, if the pastor fails to meet those expectations, he or she will not be granted the authority to introduce the changes needed to the congregation. Unfortunately, even if he or she fulfills both roles there is no guarantee that the church will implement the desired changes. As a pastor, are you willing to pay this price? Are you willing to spend the next three to five years trying to serve your church without any guarantee of success?

Change in Lay Leadership

Not only do churches require new pastoral leadership to change, but they often also require new lay leadership. Just as I had to be willing to change or get out of the way for change to happen, lay leaders must be willing to give up their positions of authority if necessary. This is usually a difficult step to take because they usually perceive themselves to be the most biblically literate or the most spiritually wise individuals in the congregations, which is why they think they should be in control in the first place. They usually have been around the longest and invested the most time and money in the life of a congregation.

Influential lay leaders will not usually volunteer to step down on their own. Often it takes intervention or confrontation.[5] They have sat on boards and committees through countless pastors who brought new ideas, and they have successfully resisted every one of them until the pastors left. They see themselves as protectors of the church and even defenders of the faith. God is on their side, in their minds, which makes them formidable opponents. For them to lose would mean that God lost, and they will use any tactic to ensure victory.

Conveniently, while they are defending God's honor, they are also protecting their turf and their power in the church. In some cases, the positions they hold have been passed down from one generation to another. In the most dysfunctional churches there may even be two or three generations of the same family sitting on the same board or committee. I know of one church where the majority of members were all from the same family. It took two years before the pastor realized that the church business meeting happened at Grandma's house two hours before anyone came to the church. This was truly a "family" church, and a very unhealthy one.

Every judicatory leader knows of churches where it is said, "There's nothing wrong with that church that a couple of funerals couldn't fix." This is sad, but true. It's sad because people are allowing controllers to hold their churches hostage to their own personal interests. It's even sadder that no one will stand up to them and put an end to it.

Borden is correct when he says that these people will not normally leave without some type of confrontation, and pastors will seldom successfully confront them. Church controllers have usually been in their positions long before a pastor arrives on the scene, and they are willing to wait until that pastor leaves. In some cases, previous pastors did confront them and lost, which merely solidified their position in the church. To successfully remove unhealthy leaders from positions of authority requires the involvement of laypeople who are committed to seeing the church move forward. It is they who must confront the controllers and challenge their hold on the rest of the church. If they don't, the church will remain in the grip of dysfunctional leaders.

The best time for this to happen is when the church is between pastors. Well-trained interim pastors can lead this process. I have been very appreciative of interims who recognized the need for some highly dysfunctional people to be removed from positions of authority before a new pastor came to the church. These interims have little to lose, and if they can recruit enough strong leaders in the church to help them, the controllers can be successfully challenged and replaced before a new pastor arrives. It is an unavoidable fact that controllers must be confronted before any significant change can occur.

Of course, some current leaders are willing to step down for the good of the congregation. A pastor told me of an elderly deacon in the church who tendered his resignation. The deacon explained that he lived through the Great Depression and approached things, especially involving money, much differently than most people currently attending the church. Even though the church was now financially strong, he could remember a time when it could barely pay its monthly bills. The church was making some financial decisions with which he was very uncomfortable, but he realized his discomfort stemmed from the experiences of his life. He did not want to be a hindrance to the church's ability to move forward and felt that he needed to step down from leadership in the church.

This deacon had faithfully served his church for four decades in just about every leadership category the church had. He was one of the true patriarchs in the church, but he realized the church now required new leadership as it entered a new cycle of ministry. He was willing to step down so the church could move forward. May his tribe increase!

Does your church need new lay leadership? As a lay leader, are you willing to pay that price? Would you be willing to step aside to allow the church to move forward with the fresh vision and leadership it needs to minister in the twenty-first century? I realize doing so may exact a great personal cost, but refusing to step aside may cost the church even more.

Conflict

Any significant change in a church will create conflict. Many people associate change with loss, and loss is always painful. Quite often they are right. Old things, such as rituals, customs, and traditions may be left behind in order to bring about the change. The loss of these, some of which are very meaningful to people in the congregation, cause individuals to grieve. That grief can lead to pain, and pain will likely lead to conflict. Unless you are ready to pay the cost associated with conflict, you should not attempt to introduce change into your church.

How is this conflict played out in a church? Gil Rendle of the Alban Institute describes what leaders might expect when people begin to react to proposed changes in their churches.

One of the dilemmas of leading change in a congregation is that it naturally engages negative and angry feelings. These negative feelings develop as general anxiety begins to increase because of the awareness of change that faces the congregation. As the anxiety increases, it begins to become more focused and people are able to identify what they fear they will lose in the change. The fear prompts the basic reaction of fight or flight that has been hardwired into all of us and into groups. It is a natural and normal response. As anxiety increases and begins to find focus, some people will stay to fight for or against the change and will express anger. Others will distance themselves from the congregation, either leaving quietly so as not to engage any further discomfort or leaving with parting shots such as "This certainly isn't what I go to church (or synagogue) for!"[6]

Fight or flight. Either reaction is costly to your church. Those who choose to stay and fight can create serious disruptions in the church. They may bring others to their viewpoint, resulting in an "us versus them" mentality. Any time people begin to choose sides it is damaging to the church. In such churches, division creates so much tension it is almost impossible to worship, and guests to your services pick up on it. They may not know what is happening in your church, but they feel the heaviness in the air and know something isn't right. It is unlikely those guests will return.

The church I pastored faced two major battles during my time there, and people chose sides. Angry words were spoken from both sides and relationships were impacted. Thankfully, the battles were fought in the open. The opposing sides recommended changes publicly and both sides presented their arguments. At times arguments became heated, but at least the issues were being discussed, and in time they were resolved. The greatest damage occurs when people agree on the surface with proposed changes but work behind the scenes to circumvent the changes.

I have seen churches experience a serious decline in financial giving because people were opposed to changes the pastor supported. In at least two churches, people admitted privately to others they were withholding financial support, hoping to force the pastor to resign. In one case, the strategy worked. The church could no longer afford to pay the minister, and he had to leave the church to support his family. Later, in a congregational meeting at that church, I was asked my thoughts about such action, and I told them it was one of the most unspiritual things I had ever heard Christian people do. I reminded them they had not just driven off their pastor because of their childish behavior but had robbed God of their tithes. Some in the church didn't appreciate my words, but they couldn't run me off because they weren't paying my salary!

If people openly oppose change, that opposition can be addressed. It is much more difficult to address opposition when it is underground. The latter can actually be more costly to a church than open warfare and indicates a serious problem in the church. It is symptomatic of a low-trust situation to believe we cannot discuss differences with one another, and low-trust churches are never healthy.

The alternative to fighting is fleeing, and people certainly do leave their churches because they oppose changes that are being discussed. In some cases, their leaving is the healthiest thing for both them and the church. Many churches get too worked up when someone threatens to leave. A church may decide to go in a direction that creates a lot of discomfort for an individual. Rather than staying to oppose a decision that a majority of the church has made, some people decide it is better for them to find another church in which they might be more comfortable. They may find it easier for them to both worship and exercise their spiritual gifts in the new church, which means they have made a good decision both for the church and for their own spiritual development.

Before beginning my pastoral ministry, our family left our church under such circumstances. The church had called a pastor with whom I personally had a good relationship, but whose theology and actions I disagreed with. For several months I had been away from the church preaching and serving a short-term interim pastorate. When the interim pastorate ended, we returned to our home church and heard a sermon that made us very uncomfortable on theological grounds. I talked to him about our concerns that Sunday afternoon and by the end of the week we decided this was a good time for us to leave the church.

The majority of the membership agreed theologically and philosophically with the pastor and were quite content with his ministry. We were not interested in challenging that, but we also could not in good conscience continue to sit under his teaching and leadership. I shared with him that I continued to appreciate him as an individual but because of my theological disagreements with him, we could not continue to attend church there. We simply never returned to that church. We found another church to attend, and a few months later I was called to be the pastor of a church in our community.

From that I learned there are valid reasons for a person to leave one church for another, and as a pastor I tried to affirm those people who left our church under such conditions. That doesn't mean it wasn't painful to see them go, but I knew that sometimes it is necessary to change churches in order to continue one's spiritual growth or to use one's gifts for ministry. It is interesting to note that the church we left had licensed me for ministry the previous year, but the pastor never allowed me to preach there because my theology was more conservative than his. As long as he remained the pastor of that church, I would never be able to develop the gifts God had given me, so God led us to another church where we could use our gifts, and I served as the pastor of that church for twenty years.

Of course, sometimes a pastor isn't sad to see certain people leave. It is easier to not have to deal with people who are always disgruntled about one thing or another or who are often in the middle of the latest conflict in the church. Sometimes the best thing that can happen to a church is for those people to leave, but that doesn't make their leaving any less costly. They can leave a lot of damage behind them, and oftentimes they continue their battle against a church in the public arena. Many unchurched people will assume the unflattering things said about a church are true, without ever asking the motives of the person making the statements. This can be very costly to a church, and almost impossible to overcome.

Can this damage be avoided? I suppose it is impossible to avoid all conflict, especially during a time of transition, but there are some common-sense steps church leaders can take to avoid its worst forms. I have discussed this topic in greater detail in two previous books,[7] so I will only briefly mention these steps here.

Move Slowly

It may take five years to fully implement significant change into your church, so take your time and do it right. Moving too quickly scares people. In recent months we've seen President Obama try to hurry Congress into passing major changes to the health care system in America. His desire for speed frightened many people. They wondered what he was trying to hide in the legislation he wanted so quickly to pass. His health care bill did finally pass, but not until people had a chance to review it and negotiate some changes to the original proposal. Pastors who try to move too quickly in implementing change in a congregation will run into the same resistance.

Enlist Supporters

It is a big mistake to announce a significant change for the first time in a congregational meeting. It is almost guaranteed that in such a setting the majority of people will be against the change. It is much wiser to share it with a few of the leaders of the church and ask for their feedback. Identify the people who are most likely to support your idea, and share it with them first. They will often ask excellent questions that will make the proposal better. They will also likely know which parts of the change will be opposed and by whom. These issues can be addressed before the plan for change is presented to the church. Once a group of leaders agree the change is needed, they will become your primary advocates. They can help explain the change to others and gain their support. By the time the pastor is ready to share it with the entire congregation, a large majority may already support it. More important than their support is that since they've had time to process it and put their stamp on it, they now own it. It's no longer just the pastor's proposal. It belongs to the church leadership, which increases the likelihood it will be implemented.

Listen to the Whispers

John Maxwell tells us to "listen to the whispers and you won't have to hear the screams."[8] Great advice! One sure way to cause conflict to escalate is to ignore others' questions and concerns. From the beginning, treat every question and concern as an opportunity to promote the change. Respond quickly and honestly to every person who raises concerns. You may think some of the issues are minor or even silly, but remember that you have already spent a lot of time thinking about this change and your questioners haven't. They need time to process it and consider the resources you used as you formulated your idea.

Stephen Covey challenges leaders to "seek first to understand, then to be understood."[9] It is essential that a leader understand the congregation's questions and concerns about the proposal, and perhaps it is even more important to understand the emotions driving those concerns. Quite often you are not dealing with a lack of understanding, you are dealing with people's feelings, fears, and pain. If you only address their questions with facts, believing that if they better understood what you are wanting to do they would support it, you will lose. To properly address their questions you must understand the emotions behind the questions. These emotions must be addressed first. If you can take away their fear, it is much more likely they will support the changes.

Create Urgency

A major reason attempts at transforming a congregation fail is that the leader did not create a sense of urgency for change.[10] Most Christians in America are not looking for change. They want stability and predictability, and significant change promises exactly the opposite.[11] Such people often live in denial. They can see the declining numbers in both attendance and finances, but they continue to operate as if nothing has changed. They seem to believe if they only work a little harder and if people would just become more dedicated that everything would once again be like it was in the "good old days." People are not going to change until they believe they have to, and a sense of urgency will clearly communicate the need for change.

I was once teaching a group of church leaders and a question was raised about why it seemed that some churches in a community are experiencing tremendous growth while a majority of churches are barely surviving. I began to talk a little about the differences in polity between those growing churches and some of our denomination's churches that are not growing. An older gentleman spoke up quickly and said that he preferred the way the churches he had attended all his life operated. At that point I asked him the Dr. Phil question: how is that working for you?

I knew the church he attended, and I knew how it was working. That church, like many others, is a shadow of its former self. The gentleman in my class also knew the answer to my question and the look on his face was one of amazement. For him at least, there was a moment of urgency to introduce some needed changes into his church, but to my knowledge he was not able to do so. The majority of people in that church are in denial and are convinced that if they only work a little harder they will once again recapture their glory days.

Pay the Price

Once you have determined the personal cost of transforming your church, you must be willing to pay it. Anyone who tries to do something for God will face some opposition. There will be opposition from those who do not understand the change. There will be opposition from those who understand the change but just don't like it. There will be opposition from those whose kingdom you are messing with. There will be opposition from people whom the enemy controls. There will be opposition from people who just love to be contrary. You probably have each of these groups in your church.[12]

People will question your leadership. They will question your motives and spirituality. Your ministry in that particular place may be in jeopardy if you continue to promote needed change that is not wanted by a majority of people. Not only will you pay a price, but your family will not be spared. They may not be subject to the same attacks you are, but they will hear people talking, and they will be quite aware of what people are saying about you and your leadership in the church.

When you are leading change, you are the point person for that organization, and people who have been in the military will tell you being on point can be very lonely. You run the risk of being shot at from both sides. "Leaders are always failing somebody. With or without authority, someone exercising leadership will be shouldering the pains and aspirations of a community and frustrating at least some people within it."[13] Sometimes both sides feel the leader is letting them down. Those seeking change may believe the leader isn't moving fast enough, while those who oppose it feel threatened by the leader's actions. It is also a fact that many people want change to occur, but only if it results in minimal loss to them, and they expect their leaders to protect their interests and minimize their losses.[14] In essence, they place their leaders in a no-win position. What is a leader to do in such circumstances?

The long-term challenge of leadership is to develop people's adaptive capacity for tackling an ongoing stream of hard problems. The point is not to foster dependency but to counteract the inappropriate dependency on authority that distress tends to produce in adaptive situations. Yet in the actual exercise of leadership, dependency must wax and wane. People need to rest the weight of their burden on someone's shoulders. How many of us manage without the hope of being protected or rescued in times of distress? Leadership requires carrying that burden and containing the distress while people adapt sufficiently to change.[15] Part of being a leader is balancing the push for change and care for those who are hurt by it. Such balancing acts are very costly to leaders. They pay a price emotionally, spiritually, and relationally. Unless leaders maintain a strong spiritual life and dependence on God, they may not be able to reach the goal. Because of this most pastors are only able to bring about one major change during their tenure at a church.[16]

Answering the Question

Now that you have considered the cost of change, are you and your church willing to pay the price to become healthy? Are you able to pay the price? If you are a pastor who is planning to move in a couple of years, you are not able to pay the price to implement the changes your church needs to become healthier. If you are a pastor who needs the church to be dependent upon you, you are not able to pay the price. You need to grow more before you are able to empower other leaders.

If a church lives in denial, it is not able to pay the price for change. It simply won't see the need for any changes and will refuse to implement them. If a church has traveled so far in its life cycle that it is near death, it probably will not be able to pay the price because it will not have the resources to do so. If a church has a history of being run by controlling factions, each of which have clearly staked out their territories, it is unlikely to be able to pay the price required for healing and growth.

Even if the leaders and the church are able to pay the price, that still doesn't answer the question of their willingness to do so. As we have seen, the cost to turn an unhealthy situation around can be enormous, and quite frankly, my experience has been that most churches and their pastoral and lay leadership are not willing to pay the price. They will give lip service to change, but when their own personal interests are affected they quickly find ways to halt the change efforts. Only those churches and leaders who are totally committed to seeing their church become healthy will pay the cost.

In the rural Indiana landscape where I live, many of our churches still hold annual revival meetings. I remember as a boy these meetings might last two weeks; now most churches schedule three-day revivals that consist of a speaker and some special music. An eighty-year-old pastor in one of my churches asked me this week my opinion of these meetings. I told him that most of them were simply meetings that people hoped would spark something good in their churches. While that is always a possibility, I think most of them fall far short of anything that could be defined as a revival. Genuine revivals are God-sent, not human made.

If a church desires genuine revival, I believe it will begin when a church decides it is willing to pay any price to once again become the church God intends it to be. If that price means having new leadership, then so be it. If that price means longtime controllers in the church must leave, then so be it. If it means that service times must change, worship styles must change, discipleship strategies must change, then so be it. If it means the church needs to relocate to better serve its community, then so be it. If it means the church needs to close its doors and hand its assets over to another church in the community that is effectively reaching people for Jesus Christ, then so be it. I believe revival can break out even as a church hands its keys over to another church in order to expand the kingdom of God.

Summary

No change will occur in the life of a church without a cost. Some of these costs are rather significant, but they are a small price to pay for a church to regain its health and enjoy a vital ministry in its community. Still, congregations and their leadership must determine whether or not they are willing to pay the price to enjoy such health. It is important to remember that even if the church is willing to pay the price, it should not expect to see the final results immediately. It takes time to regain health, and the process is often characterized by two steps forward and one step back. Just as it took me over a year to lose the weight I wanted to lose, it will take time for a church to make the changes it wants to make to become a healthier congregation, but the end result will be well worth any sacrifice and cost involved.

Epilogue to Part 2

As you've read this book, you may have identified some things about your church that trouble you. That's good! Until we identify the symptoms of disease we can go for years not knowing that there is a problem. High blood pressure is sometimes known as the silent killer because it can go undetected for years doing serious damage to vital organs. The first sign of high blood pressure is often the result of that damage unless one is proactive and has regular blood pressure checks. Heart disease is similar in that one can suffer for years with clogged arteries or other heart issues and never know it until suffering a heart attack. Such attacks are sometimes fatal, and the person has no opportunity to address the disease that caused the attack. If you have read something in this book that has identified some potential spiritual health issues in your church, consider yourself blessed. You have an opportunity to address the problem before it is fatal to your church.

Diagnosing the seriousness of the condition requires asking the tough questions found in chapter 8. It is important that you answer those questions with complete honesty. If the answers are painful, fine. This is not the time to give "spiritually correct" answers. Discuss the questions and your answers with other leaders in your church and ask for their feedback. You may also want to use the diagnostic questions I mentioned near the end of chapter 9 to further assist in the diagnosis of your church. Once your diagnosis is complete, then you can take intentional steps to address any problems you identified.

The good news for your church is that it is God's will for your church to be healthy. However, you must intentionally pursue that health. It isn't automatic, and the church must be willing to pay the price to be healthy. Changes will often have to be made, and such changes are often painful. Just as you would not make major changes in your health without the assistance of a health care provider, it's a good idea to invite someone to come alongside your church as it makes significant changes. This can be a denominational or judicatory person, a consultant, or a coach who can help lead the process that will help address the issues that are challenging the health of your church.

As you address the heart issues that may have developed over time in your congregation you will find renewed energy, a renewed purpose, and the opportunity to have a greater impact on the community God has entrusted to you. I think you'll agree that is worth any short-term cost your church may have to pay.

Notes

Introduction

1. Jill M. Hudson, *When Better Isn't Enough: Evaluation Tools for the 21st-Century Church* (Herndon, VA: Alban Institute, 2004), 17.
2. Reggie McNeal, *The Present Future: Six Tough Questions for the Church* (San Francisco: Jossey-Bass, 2003), 4.
3. George Barna, *Revolution* (Wheaton, IL: Tyndale, 2005), 13-14.

Part 1
Chapter 1

1. Eugene H. Peterson, *Eat This Book: A Conversation in the Art of Spiritual Reading* (Grand Rapids: Eerdmans, 2006), 58.
2. C. S. Lewis, *Mere Christianity* (New York: Macmillan, 1952), 40-41.
3. Josh McDowell, *Evidence That Demands a Verdict: Historical Evidences for the Christian Faith* (San Bernardino, CA: Campus Crusade for Christ, 1972), 44.
4. Frederic G. Kenyon, *Our Bible and Ancient Manuscripts* (New York: Harper and Brothers, 1941), 23.
5. McDowell, *Evidence That Demands a Verdict*, 68-75.
6. Lee Strobel, *The Case for Christ: A Journalist's Personal Investigation of the Evidence for Jesus* (Grand Rapids: Zondervan, 1998), 97.
7. David Berlinski, *The Devil's Delusion: Atheism and Its Scientific Pretensions* (New York: Basic Books, 2009), 129-30.
8. Ravi Zacharias, *Can Man Live Without God* (Nashville: W Publishing Group, 1994), 101.
9. George Barna, "Barna Survey Examines Changes in Worldview Among Christians over the Past 13 Years," The Barna Group, http:www.barna.org/barna-update/article/21-transformation/252-barna-survey-examines-changes-in-world-view-among-christians-over-the-past-13-years (accessed June 20, 2011).
10. Public Religion Research, "2008 Mainline Protestant Clergy Voices Survey FINAL Top Line Results," Public Religion Research, http://www.publicreligion.org/objects/uploads/fck/file/Clergy%20Report/LGBT%20Topline.pdf (accessed June 20, 2011).
11. Thom S. Rainer, *Surprising Insights from the Unchurched and Proven Ways to Reach Them* (Grand Rapids: Zondervan, 2001), 45.
12. Ibid.
13. Colleen Carroll, *The New Faithful: Why Young Adults Are Embracing Christian Orthodoxy* (Chicago: Loyola Press, 2002), 29.
14. Ibid., 15.
15. Larry Burkett, *The Coming Economic Earthquake* (Chicago: Moody Press, 1991).
16. Ibid., 206.

17. James T. Draper Jr., *Authority: The Critical Issue for Southern Baptists* (Old Tappan, NJ: Fleming H. Revell, 1984), 96.

18. Elmer L. Towns and Ed Stetzer, *Perimeters of Light: Biblical Boundaries for the Emerging Church* (Chicago: Moody Publishers, 2004), 179.

Chapter 2

1. Dan Kimball, *They Like Jesus but Not the Church: Insights from Emerging Generations* (Grand Rapids: Zondervan, 2007), 98.

2. Jack Van Impe, *Heart Disease in Christ's Body* (Royal Oak, MI: Jack Van Impe Ministries, 1984), 43-46.

3. Charles R. Swindoll, *The Grace Awakening* (Dallas: Word, 1990), 135.

4. Ibid., 44.

5. Kenneth L. Chafin, *The Communicator's Commentary: 1, 2 Corinthians*, vol. 7 of *The Communicator's Commentary Series*, ed. Lloyd J. Ogilvie (Waco, TX: Word, 1985), 72.

Chapter 3

1. Edward H. Hammett, *Spiritual Leadership in a Secular Age: Building Bridges Instead of Barriers* (St. Louis: Chalice Press, 2005), 69.

2. Reggie McNeal, *The Present Future: Six Tough Questions for the Church* (San Francisco: Jossey-Bass, 2003), 65.

3. Ibid., 15.

4. Dennis W. Bickers, *Intentional Ministry in a Not-So-Mega Church* (Kansas City: Beacon Hill Press of Kansas City, 2009).

5. Ed Stetzer and David Putnam, *Breaking the Missional Code: Your Church Can Become a Missionary in Your Community* (Nashville: Broadman & Holman, 2006), 40.

6. John MacArthur Jr., *The MacArthur New Testament Commentary: Romans 1-8* (Chicago: Moody Press, 1991), 352.

7. Ravi Zacharias, *Jesus Among Other Gods* (Nashville: W Publishing Group, 2000), 7.

8. Stetzer and Putnam, *Breaking the Missional Code*, 122.

9. Milfred Minatrea, *Shaped by God's Heart: The Passion and Practices of Missional Churches* (San Francisco: Jossey-Bass, 2004), 112.

10. Darrell L. Guder, *Missional Church: A Vision for the Sending of the Church in North America* (Grand Rapids: Eerdmans, 1998), 5.

11. Minatrea, *Shaped by God's Heart*, xvi.

12. Kentucky Baptist Convention, "Your Sunday School Class Can Reach Hundreds in Ten Years," http://www.kybaptist.org/kbc/blogs/ssrb.nsf/dx/07132007102251PMWEB4TC.htm (accessed October 12, 2011).

13. Stephen Gray and Franklin Dumond, *Legacy Churches* (St. Charles, IL: ChurchSmart Resources, 2009).

14. Ibid., 36.

15. Ibid., 35-36.

16. Ibid., 37.

17. Larry McKain, *Falling in Love with the Church* (Kansas City: NCS Publishing, 2004), 164-67.

Chapter 4

1. Paul D. Borden, *Hit the Bullseye: How Denominations Can Aim the Congregation at the Mission Field* (Nashville: Abingdon Press, 2003), 17.

2. Hudson, *When Better Isn't Enough*, 27-28.

3. George Barna, *A Fish Out of Water* (Nashville: Integrity Publishers, 2002), 7.

4. Tony Campolo, *Can Mainline Denominations Make a Comeback?* (Valley Forge, PA: Judson Press, 1995), 165.

5. Jackson W. Carroll, *God's Potters: Pastoral Leadership and the Shaping of Congregations* (Grand Rapids: Eerdmans, 2006), 155.

6. Bickers, *Intentional Ministry*, 102-4.

7. Thomas G. Bandy, *Fragile Hope* (Nashville: Abingdon Press, 2002), 129.

8. Roy M. Oswald, *Making Your Church More Inviting* (Bethesda, MD: Alban Institute, 1992), 6.

9. Stephen Arterburn and Jack Felton, *Toxic Faith: Understanding and Overcoming Religious Addiction* (Nashville: Oliver Nelson Books, 1991), 165-71.

10. Stephen Covey, foreword to *Servant Leadership: A Journey into the Nature of Legitimate Power and Greatness*, 25th anniversary ed., by Robert K. Greenleaf (Mahwah, NJ: Paulist Press, 2002), 3.

11. George Barna, *The Power of Team Leadership: Achieving Success Through Shared Responsibility* (Colorado Springs: WaterBrook Press, 2001), 17.

12. John C. Maxwell, *Leadership Gold: Lessons Learned from a Lifetime of Leading* (Nashville: Thomas Nelson, 2008), 77.

13. Mike Regele, *Death of the Church* (Grand Rapids: Zondervan, 1995), 95.

14. Gary R. Collins, *Christian Coaching: Helping Others Turn Potential into Reality* (Colorado Springs: NavPress, 2001), 123.

15. John C. Maxwell, *Failing Forward: Turning Mistakes into Stepping-Stones for Success* (Nashville: Thomas Nelson, 2000), 15.

16. Nancy Ortberg, *Christian Reflections on the Leadership Challenge*, eds. James M. Kouzes and Barry Z. Posner (San Francisco: Jossey-Bass, 2004), 90.

17. Leonard Ravenhill, *Why Revival Tarries* (Minneapolis: Bethany House Publishers, 1982), 110.

18. Maxwell, *Leadership Gold*, 15.

19. N. Graham Standish, *Becoming a Blessed Church: Forming a Church of Spiritual Purpose, Presence, and Power* (Herndon, VA: Alban Institute, 2005), 125.

20. Timothy C. Geoffrion, *The Spirit-Led Leader: Nine Leadership Practices and Soul Principles* (Herndon, VA: Alban Institute, 2005), 31.

21. Henry Blackaby and Richard Blackaby, *Spiritual Leadership: Moving People onto God's Agenda* (Nashville: Broadman and Holman, 2001), 164-68.

22. Bill Easum, *Put on Your Own Oxygen Mask First: Rediscovering Ministry* (Nashville: Abingdon Press, 2004), 29.

23. Doyle L. Young, *New Life for Your Church* (Grand Rapids: Baker Book House, 1989), 92-93.

Chapter 5

1. Bill Easum, *Taking Risks in Ministry*, ed. Dale Galloway (Kansas City: Beacon Hill Press of Kansas City, 2003), 93.

2. Randy Pope, *The Intentional Church: Moving from Church Success to Community Transformation* (Chicago: Moody, 2006), 82-83.

3. Cited in Charles R. Swindoll, *Improving Your Serve: The Art of Unselfish Living* (Waco, TX: Word, 1981), 29.

4. Quoted in J. I. Packer, *A Quest for Godliness: The Puritan Vision of the Christian Life* (Wheaton, IL: Crossway, 1990), 70.

5. Minatrea, *Shaped by God's Heart,* 54.

6. Erwin McManus, *An Unstoppable Force: Daring to Become the Church God Had in Mind* (Loveland, CO: Group Publishing, 2001), 71.

7. David R. Ray, *The Indispensable Guide for Smaller Churches* (Cleveland: Pilgrim Press, 2003), 133.

8. Hammett, *Spiritual Leadership,* 113.

9. Minatrea, *Shaped by God's Heart,* xvi.

10. Robert Munger, "Training the Laity for Ministry," *Theology News and Notes* (June 1973), 3.

11. Greg Ogden, *Unfinished Business: Returning the Ministry to the People of God,* rev. ed. of *The New Reformation* (Grand Rapids: Zondervan, 2003), 9.

12. Steve Ogne and Tim Roehl, *Transformissional Coaching: Empowering Leaders in a Changing Ministry World* (Nashville: B&H Publishing Group, 2008), 7.

13. Gary R. Collins, *Christian Coaching: Helping Others Turn Potential into Reality* (Colorado Springs: NavPress, 2001), 16.

14. Ogden, *Unfinished Business,* 161.

15. Jeffrey D. Jones, *Travelling Together: A Guide for Disciple-Forming Congregations* (Herndon, VA: Alban Institute, 2006), 44-45.

16. Tom Paterson, *Living the Life You Were Meant to Live* (Nashville: Thomas Nelson, 1998), 218.

17. Ogden, *Unfinished Business,* 179.

18. Ray, *Indispensable Guide,* 131.

Chapter 6

1. Tony Campolo, *Can Mainline Denominations Make a Comeback?* (Valley Forge, PA: Judson Press, 1995), 117.

2. Gallup, "Abortion," Gallup, Inc., http://www.gallup.com/poll/1576/abortion .aspx (accessed June 20, 2011).

Chapter 7

1. William Barclay, *The Gospel of Mark,* rev. ed. (Philadelphia: Westminster Press, 1956), 67.

2. John MacArthur Jr., *The MacArthur New Testament Commentary: Revelation 1-11* (Chicago: Moody Press, 1999), 111-12.

Epilogue to Part 1

1. Neil Cole, *Organic Church: Growing Faith Where Life Happens* (San Francisco: Jossey-Bass, 2005), 41.

2. Thom S. Rainer, *Breakout Churches: Discover How to Make the Leap* (Grand Rapids: Zondervan, 2005), 74.

3. Rob Phillips, "SBC Mission Giving Rises; Baptisms Fall," Baptist Press, April 23, 2009, http://www.bpnews.net/bpnews.asp?ID=30332 (accessed June 20, 2011).

Part 2
Chapter 8

1. Peter L. Steinke, *Healthy Congregations: A Systems Approach* (Herndon, VA: Alban Institute, 1996), 105.

2. Cole, *Organic Church*, xxvii.

3. *Merriam-Webster's Collegiate Dictionary*, 9th ed., s.v. "sanctuary."

4. Leonard Sweet, *Out of the Question—Into the Mystery: Getting Lost in the God-Life Relationship* (Colorado Springs: WaterBrook Press, 2004), 140.

5. Paul D. Borden, *Direct Hit: Aiming Real Leaders at the Mission Field* (Nashville: Abingdon Press, 2006), 81-82.

6. Robert N. Nash Jr., *An 8-Track Church in a CD World* (Macon, GA: Smyth & Helwys Publishing, 1997), 2.

Chapter 9

1. Steinke, *Healthy Congregations*, 10.

2. Ibid., 57.

3. Arthur Paul Boers, *Never Call Them Jerks: Healthy Responses to Difficult Behavior* (Herndon, VA: Alban Institute, 1999), 85.

4. Jonathan Falwell, *Innovatechurch* (Nashville: B&H Publishing Group, 2008), 42.

5. Rainer, *Breakout Churches*, 43.

6. Ron Blake, *The Pastor's Guide to Effective Ministry* (Kansas City: Beacon Hill Press of Kansas City, 2002), 102-3.

7. Rainer, *Surprising Insights from the Unchurched*, 120-22.

8. Standish, *Becoming a Blessed Church*, 145.

9. John C. Maxwell, *Put Your Dream to the Test* (Nashville: Thomas Nelson, 2009), 128.

10. Rick Warren, *The Purpose Driven Church* (Grand Rapids: Zondervan, 1995), 111.

11. Blake, *Pastor's Guide*, 103.

12. Stephen A. Macchia, *Becoming a Healthy Church: 10 Characteristics* (Grand Rapids: Baker Book House, 1999), 16.

13. Peter Scazzero, *The Emotionally Healthy Church: A Strategy for Discipleship That Actually Changes Lives* (Grand Rapids: Zondervan, 2003), 20.

Chapter 10

1. Quoted in Greenleaf, *Servant Leadership*, 351.

2. John C. Maxwell, *The 21 Irrefutable Laws of Leadership: Follow Them and People Will Follow You* (Nashville: Thomas Nelson, 1998), 10.

3. George Barna, *Turn-Around Churches: How to Overcome Barriers to Growth and Bring New Life to an Established Church* (Ventura, CA: Regal Books, 1993), 47.

4. Borden, *Direct Hit*, 51.

5. Borden, *Hit the Bullseye*, 73.

6. Gilbert R. Rendle, *Leading Change in the Congregation: Spiritual and Organizational Tools for Leaders* (Herndon, VA: Alban Institute, 1998), 107.

7. *The Healthy Small Church* and *Intentional Ministry in a Not-so-Mega Church*.

8. Maxwell, *Leadership Gold*, 52.

9. Stephen Covey, *The 7 Habits of Highly Effective People* (New York: Simon & Schuster, 1989), 237.

10. Jim Herrington, Mike Bonem, and James H. Furr, *Leading Congregational Change: A Practical Guide for the Transformational Journey* (San Francisco: Jossey-Bass, 2000), 35.

11. George W. Bullard Jr., *Pursuing the Full Kingdom Potential of Your Congregation* (St. Louis: Lake Hickory Resources, 2005), 25.

12. Dan Southerland, *Transitioning: Leading Your Church Through Change* (Grand Rapids: Zondervan Publishing House, 1999), 112.

13. Ronald A. Heifetz, *Leadership Without Easy Answers* (Cambridge, MA: Belknap Press of Harvard University Press, 1994), 235-36.

14. Ibid., 239.

15. Ibid., 247.

16. Anthony Pappas and Scott Planting, *Mission: The Small Church Reaches Out* (Valley Forge, PA: Judson Press, 1993), 54.

Also by Dennis Bickers

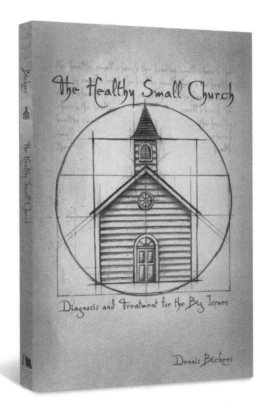

The Healthy Small Church diagnoses those things that can threaten the life of the church and prescribes practical remedies for treatment. In it, author Dennis Bickers helps your church become a healthy church that:

- Has a positive self-image
- Shares a common vision that creates purpose and unity
- Maintains community
- Practices the importance of faithful stewardship and financial support
- Encourages everyone to serve according to his or her spiritual gifts

---

The Healthy Small Church
ISBN 978-0-8341-2240-6

To order go to
www.BeaconHillBooks.com

BEACON HILL PRESS
OF KANSAS CITY

Also by Dennis Bickers

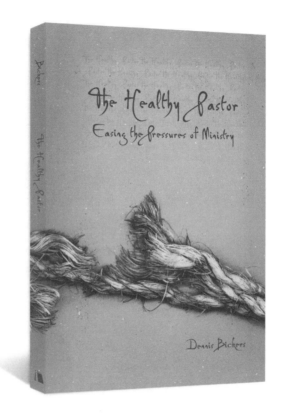

The Healthy Pastor seeks to provide insights into the expectations churches and ministers have of the pastor's role. Dennis Bickers addresses some of the common pressure points every minister experiences and provides solutions to those pressures. Ministers will be challenged to create balance in several areas of their lives: their relationship with God, family, the church, their self, and—for bivocational ministers—their second job.

The Healthy Pastor
ISBN 978-0-8341-2553-7

To order go to
www.BeaconHillBooks.com

BEACON HILL PRESS
OF KANSAS CITY